WHAT PEOPLE

"Rarely does a book come along that offers practical MBA level knowledge that energizes the soul…"

"The High Achiever Leadership Formula is perfect for two types of leaders: Leaders who have untapped potential within them and leaders who are stuck and need a breakthrough. Rarely does a book come along that offers practical MBA level knowledge that energizes the soul so that implementation begins immediately. If your desire is to unleash your leadership potential and/or get unstuck in your climb up the leadership mountain, then this book is for you."

Tom Ziglar, CEO Ziglar & Proud Son of Zig Ziglar
Ziglar.com

"Full of content and step-by-step formats…It was very easy to follow…Highly recommended!"

"I just finished "The High Achiever Leadership Formula". The book is full of content and step-by-step formats on how to become a High Achiever. I have completed the exercise in Chapter 6 - creating our Mission Statement. It was very easy to follow and made it incredibly easy to articulate what we do! Highly recommended!

Madena Parsley, CEO/Founder of Casa Sana
CasaSana.org

"Powerful tool for finding real solutions in running a successful business, be it a for-profit or not-for-profit."

"A very powerful tool for finding real solutions in running a successful business, be it a for-profit or not-for-profit. It helps take my team to the next level in doing our best in providing a brighter future for our students and schools."

Didier Aur, Development Director, Jubilee Catholic Schools Network & President, Blue Streak Scholarship Fund,
Memphis, TN
BlueStreakMemphis.net

"Gary really delivers on the promise…He actually breaks down a formula for achieving amazing results in both business and life."

"In The High Achiever Leadership Formula, Gary really delivers on the promise. He doesn't mean "formula" in some vague sense. He actually breaks down a formula for achieving amazing results in both business and life. What is often a somewhat ambiguous topic is made practical and actionable. Highly recommended for anybody looking to become a great leader!"

Josh Turner, Wall Street Journal Best Selling Author & Founder of LinkedSelling
LinkedUniversity.com

The High Achiever Leadership Formula

The 6 Ingredients of an Inspiring & Influential Leader

Gary Wilbers

ISBN: 0692777350
ISBN-13:9780692777350

DEDICATION

This book is dedicated to

Dana my wife, partner, and friend who has believed in me since the day we met.

My children Chris, Adam, and Elle who have inspired me to become a better person and Dad.

All my former educators who have inspired me to become the person I am today.

This book is written for

All my former team members and leaders who helped our companies be successful. I treasure the time you provided our companies, and my hope is I shared some knowledge with you along the way in order to help you become a better leader in your life.

CONTENTS

Introduction   vii

1 The High Achiever Mindset   1

2 The Leadership Time Solution   32

3 The Leadership Communication Loop   55

4 The Conflict Resolution System   79

5 The Influence and Trust Builder   101

6 The Strategic Organizational Playbook   120

Conclusion   141

INTRODUCTION

As I pondered how to start this book, I had to decide what I wanted you to know about me. What could I say to reassure you this isn't just another self-help book based on theory? It's important for you to understand my journey and realize I have been in your shoes and continue to experience the same struggles, pains, and excitement as you do.

As an entrepreneur and business owner for the last twenty-five years, I have taken this journey, made mistakes along the way, and come to the realization that every error made me better. A leader's goal should be continual growth, not perfection.

My journey began in college when I joined the group Students in Free Enterprise (SIFE). My marketing professor and the organization's sponsor recruited me. I wanted to be involved, but my life was hectic. I was working my way through college because as the youngest of six children, my parents weren't able to financially help. I decided to attend a SIFE meeting. SIFE promoted the free-enterprise system in our local chapters through student-designed community projects. At the end of each year, successfully completed projects competed against other colleges and universities through an oral presentation in front of a panel of judges. The projects in our local communities allowed us to meet and network with local business owners while the yearly competitions allowed us to network with national leaders such as Sam Walton with Walmart and Ross Perot with Perot Systems. It was the national competitions that introduced me to a whole new world of possibilities and changed my life's direction.

Upon graduating college I knew I wanted to own my own business, but I realized I needed a "real" job utilizing my double major in Business Administration and Marketing. It was frustrating; I interviewed and interviewed. Either it was a dead-end position with no opportunity for advancement, or I didn't have enough experience. How was I to get experience if I wasn't given an opportunity?

I decided to utilize some of my connections through SIFE and contacted a Walmart executive about their Manager Trainee Program. I went through their extensive interview process only to discover I would need to relocate every six months for the first two years and then every year or two once becoming a store manager. I was offered the position, but I realized this life style was not for me. I turned it down.

I finally secured an outside sales position with a local precast concrete company. I would be traveling throughout the mid-Missouri area selling precast concrete items to contractors. I have to tell you the precast concrete term sounded so much better than telling you I was actually selling septic tanks. I really enjoyed meeting new people and getting to understand the business. As construction slowed for the winter, I realized my chances of being laid off were high since I was the only nonfamily member within the company. At least I now had some experience in sales, or so I thought.

I contacted an employment agency, and they scheduled me for an interview with a mobile phone store coming to town. It was my dream job: sales manager for a new cutting-edge product, a great salary, car allowance, commissions, and bonuses. As one of two final candidates, I was heartbroken and devastated when I did not get the position. The reason: not enough sales experience. UGH! Looking back this may have been God deciding he had other things in mind for me.

As it turned out, the mobile phone industry was starting to boom, and I secured a position with another new startup but with a difference: straight commission. That meant if I sold a phone, I got paid; if I didn't, I was working for free. Remember: I was recently out of college, living on my own, had student loans to repay, and had to decide by Monday. So I sought advice from my girlfriend and future wife Dana. She has been my partner in life, business, and best friend for twenty-two years. Coincidentally, that week's Bible reading was "Don't trust in yourself, but trust in the Lord." I decided to move forward and trust this opportunity. I accepted the position on Monday and started two weeks later by going to St. Louis for a week's training about how cellular technology worked and how to install the systems. I firmly believe how we accept opportunities and proceed determines who and what we become.

When I shared my new venture with my parents, Dad's first question was, "What's a mobile phone?" After my explanation his second question was, "Why would anyone want one of those?" I told him all the facts and benefits I had learned about the technology and this new market. However, it was his last question that really set me off. "What are you being paid?" I knew his conservative values would not understand, and when I replied straight commission, his response was one of disbelief that I could be so inept to think I could make a living selling mobile phones. His indecisiveness only served to fuel my resolve to make this business a success.

Looking back these challenges, questions, and doubts were preparing me for life as an entrepreneur. A strong desire for success, a can-do attitude, and the tenacity to continue are necessary for facing challenges.

I became not only a good salesperson but also the sales manager and then the owner of that mobile phone business. It was the beginning of my career as an entrepreneur. Over the years I have owned several businesses such as soft-sided hot tubs, a marketing company, and a travel agency and have had a few business partners. I've learned how to write business plans for bank loans, deal with inventory, project sales and operating expenses, etc. Mistakes have been my greatest learning tool. My first "expensive" mistake was to invest all of the hot tub sales profit into setting up a store front assuming advertising would drive sales through our doors. While the soft-sided hot tubs were very popular when my business partner and I went to trade shows and events, it was not the same in a store front. Over the next several months we spent all the profits and did not have any new business.

Another lesson learned involved dealing with business partners. One particular incident centered around two bank loans my partner and I had. Since we were responsible business men, we paid off our loans rapidly and then celebrated being debt free. What should have been a positive was probably the death of our partnership. It changed each of our perspectives and expectations. I wanted to continue to grow the mobile phone business while my partner started investing in real estate to make additional profit. I felt as though I was doing most of the work to make the mobile phone company successful while he was working to increase his personal income.

A supportive business partner is crucial for success, and my wife Dana has always been there for me. Dana did not always agree with my crazy ideas, but she has always supported me and still does today. Over the next eighteen years we grew our wireless business to over one hundred fifty employees and fifteen locations in Missouri. In 2012, I decided to sell my wireless business plus five additional small businesses so I could fully dedicate my life to coaching, training, and keynote speaking. My plan is to help other small business owners succeed as entrepreneurs.

Over the years I have had multiple business challenges in the areas of people, productivity, and profits. This book is my framework for helping you navigate these challenges as a leader. The High Achiever Leadership Formula will guide you as you strive to understand the common challenges facing most leaders of organizations. You will learn to develop a climber mindset, create a winning game plan, and engage culture within your organization. These six chapters will help you become an inspiring and influential leader.

ACKNOWLEDGMENTS

I am deeply grateful to Rod, Melissa, Tamara, Paige, and Peggy who helped my dream of writing my first book become a reality. I want each of you to know how much I appreciate your efforts.

Rod, you are a very talented individual who is always willing to tackle new projects. I appreciate all your research and editing with the development of this book. I am thankful for all the efforts you provide Ascend Business Strategies.

Melissa, you have not been with our company very long, but your dedication and efforts have helped complete this project. I appreciate all you have done to help me realize this dream. You are an amazing individual and a great asset to our organization.

Tamara, you were a driving force as I made the change from owning multiple businesses to redefining my purpose in life and becoming a coach, trainer, and keynote speaker. I appreciate all your contributions for moving my ideas forward. You are a talented person.

Paige, you joined our company this summer as an intern and have become a valuable team member. You are a great graphic designer, and I love the book cover. You have a bright future ahead of you.

Peggy, you are a true friend, and I appreciate your work with editing and producing this book. Your inspiration in high school helped me become the leader I am today as you saw the leadership in me before I did. I can never repay you for your contribution to my life.

1

The High Achiever Mindset

"You can either have a climbing or a stuck mindset; the choice is up to you."

-Gary Wilbers

"I was totally surprised by the announcement that they were closing our location. We had been working overtime the last few months, and our workload did not seem to be letting up. The company announced it was reorganizing and decided our location would be closing. In complete shock and disbelief I realized that in ninety days I would not have a job."

My friend, an employee of the company, shared this with me during lunch. He had been with the company since graduating high school nineteen years ago. Surprised by the news, my friend became proactive as he already began formulating a plan to address the challenges ahead. I shared with him The High Achiever Mindset, and we discussed how he could implement these new strategies in order to get his desired results. In this chapter I will discuss The High Achiever Mindset so you may achieve your goals in both your personal and professional life. As I reflect on my life, I realize the mindset I created for myself has contributed to my success. The last several years of coaching, keynote speaking, and training have given me the realization that the framework I created will benefit you.

The High Achiever Mindset has a very simple formula:

Energy + Connections + Influence + Integrations = Great Results/Purpose of Life

Let's begin with a simple review of each area:

Energy

The key to energy is realizing the growth you need to exhibit in this area. Leadership is made up of our daily choices. The attitude we show to others and display in our relationships determines who we are and will become. Every day you need energy to fuel the change you desire. Execution which equals productivity allows us

2

to achieve the results we seek in our personal and professional life. We must visualize our positive mindset to achieve our daily goals.

Connections

Our interactions within our relationships decide if we are a giver or taker. True leadership is the willingness to give of ourselves and not expect anything in return.

Influence

Influence is developed by the contributions we give to others. When we are committed to helping others grow, our daily leadership has a positive influence on others. If we don't show our leadership, we become a negative influence in both their lives and ours. Having a foundation of trust with others increases our influence.

Integration

Integration is the willingness to change yourself by creating new habits and disciplines in order to become the person you want to be. It allows our relationships to grow and expand with those who are most important to us.

Great Results/Purpose Of Life

As you implement these daily strategies, you will find not only greater results but also a purposeful, fulfilling life. Napoleon Hill says, "You are the master of your destiny. You can influence, direct, and control your own environment. You can make your life what you want it to be."

MY STORY

I have been a successful entrepreneur the majority of my life, but in 2002, I realized things weren't right. Because I defined success as money, title and status, I never had enough. I was always searching for more. I thought these three things would make me happy, but happiness became a revolving door. The amount of energy I needed each day was huge. I created goals but accomplishing them didn't provide happiness. I could not satisfy my desire to be happy. I thought I was an overachiever. In reality, I felt empty. That emptiness was the driving force behind my need for more. I felt like a hamster in an exercise wheel spinning out of control.

I knew I needed to change my direction or I would lose everything-- my spouse, family, and businesses. One area in which I excelled was the desire to gain knowledge by learning new ways for self-improvement. I began developing a framework to rebuild my life. I knew I had to improve my energy, connections, and influence. I thought I could accomplish this by integrating a few new habits. It sounded simple, but I soon realized it wasn't. It was necessary to develop strategies, now known as The High Achiever Mindset, to become a new me. Through this I learned success is not acquiring things but the leadership we give to ourselves and others.

MINDSET

Mindset is defined as a particular way of thinking; a person's attitude or set of opinions about something; a mental attitude or inclination; a fixed state of mind. Changing your mindset is not easy because it has been set over a period of time, and the subconscious part of your brain will say no to new mental thinking. It takes a powerful force for you to overcome this fixed state. Can it be done? Of course, but you must create discipline with your new mindset and decide to make it your new way of thinking.

On November 18, 2002, I had another mindset change that altered my direction. As I look back, I realize 2002 was the turning point in my life. I had been working with a business coach that year, and we started the process of planning the goals I wanted to achieve in 2003. I asked my coach, "Why can't I get myself to achieve the goal of losing weight?" I was a walking heart attack at 275lbs. with a family

of three small children and a growing business. My coach responded with something I will never forget, "First, you need to schedule your training just as you do with any other appointment." He said, "Let me ask you a question: Do you miss an appointment if you have it scheduled?" I replied, "No, unless an emergency comes up." He said, "That is the way you need to respond for your training sessions." He picked up the phone, talked to someone at the gym, and scheduled my orientation session for the next Tuesday at 6 A.M. Then he said, "You must find an accountability partner to hold you responsible for attending your training sessions. I will be your accountability partner until it becomes your new mindset." Each week I would let him know when my training sessions were scheduled. After each session I would call him, or he would call me for accountability. After about three months he began to check with me weekly. After six months it

was a new habit, and I had lost over 35 lbs. On October 18, 2003, I had lost 75 lbs. My new eating and exercising plans allowed me to accomplish this in eleven months. I was in my mid-thirties when I did this, so my metabolism was stronger than it is today. I am happy to report thirteen years later, I have not only kept the weight off but improved my health.

The key objective I had to overcome was my mindset. When I changed my mindset to healthy eating and exercising, the results were amazing. We must realize our mindset has a direct impact on our results.

That one decision created a tremendous amount of success for me and was a pivotal point that changed my life. The High Achiever Mindset is a framework that started from a decision to lose some weight in order to be around for my children and to enjoy my life by being an active Dad. My children are now teenagers.

To really understand this framework, you need to evaluate your life as if you are simultaneously looking through a pair of glasses with two very different lenses.

Let's title the left lens "your viewpoint." Ask yourself these questions:

- How will I apply this to my life?
- What changes do I need to implement for improvement?
- Who can help me become better in each of these areas?

The right lens is titled "leadership." What do you want to portray to those who are important to you? Ask yourself how you show leadership in these four areas:

- Energy
- Connections
- Influence
- Integration

Am I helping others obtain what they are seeking? Am I willing to mentor others on their journey?

Do you see the difference? The left lens is about you, and the right lens is about others and what you bring to their lives. When you view your life through these lenses, your actions, habits and disciplines will change. If you are willing to fully implement The High Achiever Mindset into your daily life, you will see great results and living your purpose of life.

When I speak about The High Achiever Mindset, I point out that usually most individuals are in one of two mindsets: climber mindset or stuck mindset. Let's define these two types of mindsets:

Climber Mindset

The climber mindset is searching to grow, learn, change, and become who you want to be. As the climber you can change and grow no matter what stage of life you are in. In this mindset you are always finding new ways to accomplish goals and are willing to keep trying even when you fail. You realize your ascension in life is about continuing to grow each day.

Stuck Mindset

The stuck mindset is never wanting to fail. You always stay on the safe path and are unwilling to grow, learn, or change. You talk about the past and why the future is never going be any better. The stuck mindset always tells why it cannot be done.

Which mindset are you right now? The good news is you can create the climber mindset in your life. When we look first to ourselves, it allows us to visualize and internalize what we need to accomplish. The four pillars of energy, connection, influence, and integration then link us to the leadership we will need to share in each of these areas. Our choices, attitudes, habits, and disciplines will determine if we are truly showing leadership daily.

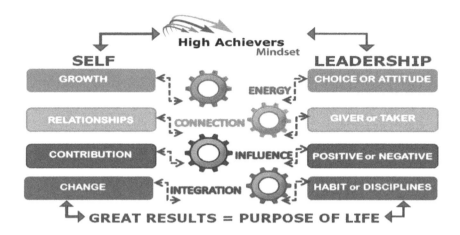

ENERGY

The first pillar is energy. It helps us look at our purpose and determines why it is important to our mindset. Energy is a choice we make daily that impacts our purpose in all aspects of life such as marriage, family, work, etc. Many of you made the choice today to be energetic and productive. Let's look at your attitude: Do you see your life as a full or empty glass?

"Your choices make your attitude, and your attitude creates your choices."

-Gary Wilbers

Energy is all about the growth you want in your life in the two areas of exercise and productivity.

Exercise

Exercise is the fuel that energizes us. Positively tuning our body becomes a holistic approach causing us to look at ways to better take care of ourselves daily. Common sense is not always common practice when it comes to our health. With the amount of information available, it is unbelievable that nearly one-third of the world's population is obese. Here are some simple steps you can easily implement to increase your overall energy level:

Physical

- Get seven-to-eight hours of sleep per night.
- Walk outside every day for a minimum of thirty minutes.
- Workout a minimum of three-to-five times a week focusing on the full body and cardio.
- Do deep breathing exercises three times a day.
- Meditate daily.

Nutritional

- Take a multi-vitamin as well as Vitamin D and Omega 3 Fish Oil.
- Drink a minimum of half your body weight in ounces of water.
- Minimize or eliminate sugary drinks, alcohol, and caffeine.
- Start each day with a healthy breakfast.
- Don't DIET! Change your eating habits to reflect a healthy lifestyle.

Daily Boosts

- Try to make everyone you interact with smile or laugh.
- Stand and stretch for three-to-five minutes for each hour of sitting.
- Focus on being completely PRESENT with no distractions in all conversations.

- Create Peak Productivity Times daily (two-to-three ninety-minute sessions with no distractions).
- Take your lunch break outside when possible or meet a friend.

(Please note these are general recommendations. You should always consult your doctor or trained health advisor before making any changes to your diet, health plan, or lifestyle.)

I suggest you take a look at each of these three areas. Which ones are you already doing? Decide now which new one from each list will you start doing today? Remember: The key is accountability. Who will you ask to hold you accountable to implement this new change? If you implement one of these energy boosters from each category in the next ninety days, you will see your energy level increase. Implement two from each category, and you will see a total energy-level transformation. Your willingness becomes your first leadership test.

Our leadership is tested each day by the attitude we show. We all get excited about starting something new, but it seems the challenge is to complete it. This description has stuck with me throughout the years because this is the key ingredient for making the difference as you move forward:

John Swindoll (n.d.) wrote: The longer I live, the more I realize the impact of attitude on life. Attitude, to me, is more important than facts. It is more important than the past, the education, the money, than circumstances, than failure, than successes, than what other people think or say or do. It is more important than appearance, giftedness or skill. It will make or break a company... a church... a home. The remarkable thing is we have a choice everyday regarding the attitude we will embrace for that day. We cannot change our past... we cannot change the fact that people will act in a certain way. We cannot change the inevitable. The only thing we can do is play on the one string we have, and that is our attitude. I am convinced that life is 10% what happens to me and 90% of how I react to it. And so it is with you... we are in charge of our Attitudes.

Productivity

The second part of energy is in the area of productivity. According to The Power of Full Engagement, (Schwartz & Loehr, 2004), Energy is the fundamental currency of high performance, not time. It has changed how we look at our energy and what we have because it changes our performance in each area of our life. The hours in our days are fixed, but the quantity and quality of available energy is not. It is our most precious resource. The more we take responsibility for the energy we bring to the world, the more empowered and productive we become.

In "The Leadership Time Solution" (Chapter 2), I will give you some practical applications about how you can improve your productivity by using the "Daily Dashboard," "My Weekly Plan," and "Habit Maker." These tools will enhance your productivity and increase your energy level. Our productivity is rooted in the amount of energy we produce each day. Multiple publications state that Tuesday is the most productive day of the week. If that is the case, do you plan your week so that Tuesday is your most productive day? I used to hold staff meetings with my direct reports on Tuesday. When I found out this was the most productive day of the week, I moved my staff meetings to Monday. Small changes in your behavior alter how productive you are in the workplace.

Do you feel that you have the same energy level in the afternoon as you do in the morning? I attended a conference recently in which the speaker spoke about how he handles his afternoon energy. He explained that he spends fifteen-to-twenty minutes meditating before he starts his work. I decided to try this productivity habit. I already had a recliner in my office but very seldom used it because I saw it as a sign of laziness. I set my phone alarm for twenty minutes. The first day it did not do much for me. For a week I did not do it again. One day I felt low on energy and decided to try it again for five days straight. I was pleasantly surprised how good I felt after I had rested each day. I started to see a pattern: My afternoon energy level was increasing, and I was accomplishing more. Strategies such as these and the ones from the first section of this chapter can change your energy level. The key is to have a climber mindset and try some.

In The Power of Full Engagement, Loehr and Schwartz state:

(Schwartz & Loehr, 2004) To be fully engaged, we must be physically energized, emotionally connected, mentally focused and spiritually aligned with a purpose beyond our immediate self-interest. Full engagement begins with feeling eager to get to work in the morning, equally happy to return home in the evening and capable of setting clear boundaries between the two. It means being able to immerse yourself in the mission you are on, whether that is grappling with a creative challenge at work, managing a group of people on a project, spending time with loved ones or simply having fun. Full engagement implies a fundamental shift in the way we live our lives. (p. 5)

My goal with writing this book is to give you guidance about how you can implement these six ingredients to become an inspiring and influential leader in both your personal and professional life. The challenge you have now is to decide what strategies you will implement within the next twenty-four hours.

Regardless of what goals you set in life, it takes determination and consistency to make them a successful reality. You must have energy. It is something you have to manufacture within yourself to stay focused and move forward. These seven key strategies will help you stay focused:

- Avoid exaggerations and negatives.
- Immediately stop negative energy.
- Focus on the positive.
- Realize it is okay to make mistakes.
- Mix with positive people.
- Be grateful.
- Focus on the present.

Brendon Burchard (LLC, 2008) states, "The power plant doesn't have energy; it generates it." Energy is the fuel for your life. We must create the climber mindset for growth and show our leadership through our choices and attitude. Is it easy? No.

CONNECTIONS

Our second pillar is based on connections. We must create high quality connections in our personal and professional life.

Professional Connections

High-quality connections is the term used to designate short-term, dynamic, and positive interactions at work. The positivity of high-quality connections is how you feel for persons involved, what they do, and the beneficial outcomes produced. For example, the uplift felt when someone expresses genuine concern for how you are after a grueling meeting or work shift.

The foundation for a high-quality connection is based on three areas: cognitive, emotional, and behavioral mechanisms which explain how to determine the level of connection. Work connections is defined as the dynamic energy existing between two people when there is some interaction involving mutual awareness.

First, we assume humans are intrinsically social and have a need to belong. Second, while we interact with each other, the connections are dynamic and change as individuals alter how they feel, think, and behave. Third, we know the work of organizations is performed through social processes, and connections are key elements for the understanding of how work is accomplished. Fourth, we assume connections vary in quality. Differences in quality reflect variance in how healthy and well-functioning the relationship is at a particular point in time.

One differentiation is the positivity of the people involved and the emotional experiences of each individual in the connection. The second impacts the connection that enhances the potentiality and the responsiveness. Positive experiences impact the vitality of feelings in the connection. People who have high-quality connections feel positive stimulus and a heightened sense of positive energy. Being positive denotes a sense of feeling known and loved or being respected and cared for in the connection. This allows for both people to feel movement in the connection and exposes vulnerability and responsiveness when full participation is experienced.

Connectivity describes a connection level of openness to new ideas and influences. High-quality connections also facilitate individual's recovery and adaption when employees are suffering from loss or illness thus undergoing transitions in their career or jobs. High-quality connections are important as a means by which people develop and grow and are also associated with greater levels of psychological safety and trust. Higher levels of interpersonal trust can enhance cooperation and trustworthiness.

Cognitive emotions highlight how conscious and unconscious thought processes predispose people to building high-quality connections. Emotional actions point out how feelings open people up to connection and are shared between people in ways that build high-quality connections. Behavioral actions determine how the two parties interact and share ideas and concerns.

Positive emotions broaden our thinking and help build durable, social resources. Gratitude or thankfulness occurs when an individual perceives that someone intentionally provides something valuable to another. Feeling grateful towards others boosts attention to the positive qualities of both parties. It should also be noted that when positive emotions are shared, the person receiving the emotions unconsciously mirrors the emotions of the other person.

A list of ways to positively connect employees to its leadership:

- Explain the overall organizational purpose and how each employee's job relates.
- Include employees in the hiring process and let them help determine who is a good fit for the organization thus building connection and trust.
- Be transparent and share things with employees.
- Build an atmosphere in which employees have open communications.
- Focus on developing employees helps them connect with the organization.
- Push employees in a positive direction in relation to job skills vs. knowledge.
- Understand each employee's communication style.
- Focus on internal customer service as much as external customer service.
- Teach people to develop and take risks in your organization.
- Disseminate information to all employees.
- Motivate and create a sense of teamwork through teambuilding.

Personal Connections

We are not as connected with people as we were just twenty years ago. Yes, we have more ways to connect through social media and the internet; we can even call people around the world without being charged a long distance fee. However, the real truth is we are less connected with society as a whole today than in the past.

For example, during my high school years in the early 1980s, we did not have wireless phones, internet, or social media. If I wanted to connect with someone, I had to either physically go see or call them on the landline phone. I realize I'm talking about something thirty plus years ago, but I don't feel as though it has been that long. Then our connection with each other was mostly face-to-face. I would spend hours at a time on the phone with someone I connected with such as a girlfriend. These connections grew because of the time we spent together as friends hanging out and participating in mutually enjoyable activities.

Today the challenge with wireless phones, internet, and social media is we can connect to people around the world in a second, but we are not intimately connected to our family and friends. Why is this? My belief is since we are bombarded with so many distractions, we have allowed these to consume and override our basic desire for human face-to-face contact. We put off connecting with those closest to us choosing instead a faster immediate gratification provided by social media. Is this really creating the communication we need or want in our life?

Communication is a compilation of traditional verbal and non-verbal elements. A study by Albert Mehrabian, author of <u>Silent Messages</u>, (Mehrabian, 1972) found only 7% of any message we receive is actually conveyed through words, 38% is through our tone of voice or style, and 55% is through our facial expressions and body language. His findings support the theory that the majority of communication is non-verbal. While social media is technically non-verbal, you might then be tempted to believe it qualifies for 93% of communication, but in no way can it convey a person's tone, facial expressions, or body language.

If we want strong, high-quality connections in our personal life, we must realize that our communication with those most meaningful to us needs to be our top priority. Remember: To have a High Achiever Mindset, your connections are an important part to living the life you want.

Follow this three-part plan to help you connect daily with those closest to you:

- Disconnect from technology and use face-to-face conversation.
- Keep your breakfast and dinner tables free from electronic gadgets.
- Don't multi-task when you are communicating with someone.

The true art of connection is being lost, but if you take the time to share your undivided attention with those closest to you, you will never regret it.

Empathy is the ability to identify and understand another's situation, feelings, and motives. It is our capacity to recognize the concerns of others. Empathy keeps relationships running smoothly as it allows us to create bonds of trust, gives insights into what others may be feeling or thinking, helps understand how or why others are reacting to situations, sharpens our insights, and informs our decisions.

Ten ways for building empathy:

- Listen.
- Don't interrupt.
- Tune in to non-verbal communication.
- Practice the "93% rule" (See study above by Albert Mehrabian).
- Use person's name.
- Be fully present.
- Smile.
- Encourage.
- Give genuine recognition and praise.
- Take personal interest.

The more we use empathy, the stronger it becomes. Try some of these suggestions and watch the reactions of others. I believe you will see some positive results in both your personal and professional relationships.

INFLUENCE

The third pillar in the High Achiever Mindset is influence. Our influence is either positive or negative. Ask yourself: What is the influence I want to show to those who are most important to me?

Personal Influence

We can all look back and find that one person who made an impact on our life. Take a moment, close your eyes, and think about that person. Mentally capture the person and visualize how he/she made a difference and influenced you. That influence has driven you to who you are today.

My mom was that person in my life. She was born in 1931 and lived through some of the most challenging times in American history. She came from a broken, poor family, but these trials made her into a caring, compassionate, and loving woman. She shared her values of faith, family, and love with her children and grandchildren. She sacrificed for each of us and always told us if we wanted something in life, we must work to attain it. My mom was a competitive person in cards, games, and life. She enjoyed her family, friends, and traveling. She believed in her faith and prayed the rosary to give her comfort and peace. My mom passed away in November 2014, but her influence will be with me for a lifetime.

As I look at my life, I wonder what type of influence I have with my family and friends. Our life is not made of what we get but instead of what we give. I was reading a story from Guideposts that talked about Danny Thomas, founder of St. Jude's Children's Hospital in Memphis, TN. (Thomas, 2016) He stated, "There are two kinds of people in the world: givers and takers. The takers may eat better, but the givers sleep better." Take time right now and inventory the influence you are giving to your most important relationships. Write down the most important relationships in your life such as spouse, children, other family members, friends, and co-workers.

To become a giver in these relationships, ask yourself these questions:

- Am I giving quality time to each of these relationships?
- Am I present when I am with these relationships?
- Do I give or take more from these relationships?
- What action do I need to take today to let these relationships know how important they are to me?
- When was the last time I genuinely thanked these relationships for who they are and what they mean to me?

Write your answers in a journal or type them on your computer. Then over the next several days, reflect and contemplate about what you wrote. My last challenge is for you to become the influence you want to be in each of these relationships. As you share of yourself, you will see your influence come back multiplied.

Professional Influence

People want to follow leaders who have a vision of where their company is going and how they uniquely contribute to the overall success. If employees are fully engaged, they share in the dreams and goals of the organization. This allows them to take ownership in executing the vision of the company. Leaders often think sharing their vision once a year at a company meeting is enough, but to create true influence in your organization, you must share your vision daily.

As organizations become increasingly global, the ability to influence others has become a must for leaders. When working across functions and geographies, leaders are often expected to produce results through people over whom they have no direct authority. Influence is turning your agenda into their agenda by gaining the commitment of others rather than forcing compliance.

Influential leaders must become more agile in their interpersonal relationships. They want to employ the full range of influencing others' behaviors which will enable them to project a new, more powerful image. They need to learn how to measure key colleagues, potential partners, fence-sitters, and adversaries and how to develop strategies for positioning their ideas and plans for acceptance by each group.

Influence is more about self-awareness and the degree to which leaders are viewed as a powerful, influential leading force in their organization. This is accomplished by learning communication techniques for modifying or changing their image and becoming a stronger force without a commanding tone. Influence is also about understanding and navigating organizational politics or forces. Developing important degrees of cooperation from key colleagues is essential. Leaders need to develop an influence plan that enables them to achieve results from across the organization.

A list of ways to influence your team:

- Empower workers to complete tasks and hold them accountable.
- Develop systems for complete accountability.
- Build and work continually with maintaining trust.
- Make decisions based on the good of the organization, not just a select few.
- Learn how to effectively delegate to your team.

- Remove the barriers for your team's success.
- Identify and reward positive behaviors.
- Include your team with scheduling.
- Conduct honest, open performance evaluations every ninety days.
- Inspect that all leaders are conducting accountability with their teams.

The influence in your team grows when you increase engagement with them. When you win over the hearts and minds of your team members, you will see them lead in ways that will lead your company to extraordinary efforts which in turn will lead to positive financial results. According to officevibe.com ("10 shocking stats about disengaged employees," 2014), engaged employees are 87% less likely to leave an organization. To influence your employees, be a visionary leader for your team and share the good and the bad. When you are willing to be vulnerable and show everything, your team will rally for helping create success in your organization. Vision can't stand alone; it must be supported with accountability for everyone on the team.

"Influence is the ability to persuade others to make a difference without them realizing it was your influence."

-Gary Wilbers

As we close this section, here are five principles of influence that will make a difference in your professional relationships:

- Enlarge people by learning.
- Navigate people from experience.
- Connect with people by understanding the art and science of leadership.

- Empower and develop people.
- Duplicate other leaders.

This topic is covered in more in (Chapter 5) "The Influence and Trust Builder."

INTEGRATION

The final pillar in The High Achiever Mindset is integration. The key to successfully implementing integration is to first look at yourself. Integrating new habits and disciplines can be hard. You must first decide to change and then set up a system to implement.

Personal Integration

According to Charles Duhigg, author of <u>The Power of Habit</u>, (Duhigg, 2012) the process within our brains is a three-step loop: First, there is a cue and a trigger tells your brain to switch into automatic mode and then signals it to which habit to use. Then there is a physical, mental, or emotional routine. Lastly, there is a reward which helps your brain determine if this particular loop is worth remembering in the future.

For example, I changed a habit which involved my morning routine. I decided I wanted to spend spiritual time each morning, read for thirty minutes, and meditate for thirty minutes. I struggled to fully implement this into my daily routine. Some days were more successful than others. I did parts of it most days but found it difficult to create the habit of completing it daily. I finally decided one day to declare my intention in a blog post. That became my accountability.

My detailed plan:

- Rise by 5 A.M. every weekday
- Create a specific space in the house
- Spend thirty minutes in spiritual time through reading, reflecting, and journaling
- Read thirty minutes of business development books
- Spend thirty minutes meditating and journaling my thoughts

I implemented this using "The Habit Loop" (Duhigg, 2012):

My CUE is the alarm clock going off at 4:50 A.M. every morning prodding me to get up, wash my face, and drink two glasses of water to energize my brain.

My ROUTINE is scheduling and completing ninety minutes of reading, reflecting, meditating, and journaling.

My REWARD is the balance of spiritual, social, and emotional wellbeing.

The hardest part is starting the new habit and then creating the inner drive for accomplishment. I will discuss in more detail the use of "The Habit Maker" in "The Leadership Time Solution" (Chapter 2). I used this process to help make my new routine become a habit and discipline. It took me multiple tries before it became a habit. Now I do it each weekday morning. According to Charles Duhigg (Duhigg, 2012), the habit loop reveals a basic truth. The brain no longer fully participates in decision making when a habit emerges. So unless you intentionally battle a habit and discover new routines, the pattern will progress automatically. Determine a habit you want to change and use "The Habit Loop" to help you through the process.

Professional Integration

Integration is an extremely analytical, process-result oriented way of making decisions. Integration is about creating a culture which builds a direct, open, honest communication channel for all employees. Integration is about developing processes and systems that set the climate for performance of the organization in terms of expectations of individuals and departments.

It would be foolish to establish a one-size-fits-all system for a company. It just does not work that way in today's workplace. The workplace of today wants total accountability that strives to keep employees informed in all areas of the business. Organizations need to be transparent in their actions and beliefs.

Five keys that must be understood in the organization:

- Have a clear, realistic shared vision.
- Understand the differences between employees and management.
- Know the people—understand their fears and concerns.
- Define and implement the processes and tools.
- Engage the workers.

Leadership needs to perform due diligence when communicating issues to employees. Employees will find out information about the organization before management is prepared to share if you do not have a communication plan. Do not ever lie to your employees. When you can, share the information with them. It is imperative you do this. Holding back information only decreases the levels of integration within an organization and impacts employee loyalty and trust.

A list of integrations you should implement into your organization:

- Have clearly defined processes.
- All meetings should tie to goals/objectives of the organization.
- Monitor and communicate the budget.
- Communicate and track the Key Performance Indicators (KPIs).
- Address issues in timely manner.
- Update your processes and accountability as needed.
- Support ongoing training both personally and professionally of your team.
- Empower your team.
- Have clear accountability.
- Follow through with promises.

As you implement these integrations into your organization, you will see engagement with your team improve. The goal is to increase engagement of each person on the team. The team will then drive your culture which in turn will drive the results of the organization.

GREAT RESULTS

"If it weren't for bad luck, I'd have no luck at all." Does your life resemble this? Why is it some people have all the luck? There are people always achieving something bigger and grander than you. You are the unluckiest person in the world and never get a break.

This is how I would have described my early professional life. No matter how hard I worked, sixty-to-eighty hours a week, I wasn't getting ahead. I was raised with the mentality that if I wanted success, it was up to me and it would take a lot of hard work. I am still not sure how this equated to luck, but it made sense at the time I was striving for great results.

Productivity was based on how many hours I worked versus the quality or quantity of my output. Delegate? No way. I wasn't comfortable with that. It was my responsibility to make sure things were done right. I micro-managed my employees at every level. I was a manager, not a leader. After one particular stressful day I realized I could not continue on this path. I began reading The 7 Habits of Highly Effective People by Stephen Covey (Covey, 1989) and became obsessed with becoming a better leader and person by following the seven habits.

Over the years I started creating my own framework for achieving great results. That framework has now become "The High Achiever Mindset" that I speak, train, and coach others about.

"Great results are generated from your energy, connections, influence you give, and integrations you adopt."

-Gary Wilbers

As you read this book, be a constant learner and knowledge seeker. We all have the capacity to learn and grow, but we must be willing to water and fertilize ourselves before we will see growth. Think of one thing you can start doing today that will make a difference in achieving the results you want. Write it down and create an action plan integrating this new behavior. Overcome the challenge by making it a habit or discipline. We are all capable of transforming our life, but we must first commit to it. Our great results will come from using the wisdom and knowledge we gain in a positive manner. My mantra: CHARGE (Create Habits Around Real Goals Everyday). You have every ability to become the person you want to be.

Purpose Of Life

Do you know who you are? Not who you say you are, but who you truly are. In other words, does the person on the inside match the person on the outside? Since I sold my businesses to go into coaching, training and keynote speaking, I have been on a quest to define my purpose of life. I have realized that I achieved this part of my life by setting goals and taking action to make them a reality. I believe this is a vital component to creating success in life. I have also realized to get greater clarity into who I am, I must define myself in two key areas: self and the leadership I show.

I asked myself these questions:

- How do I want to live my life every day?
- What do I want to be remembered for?
- What do others say about who I am?
- Am I being the person I want to be?

The first thing I did was realize I needed to refine my mission statement from 2006 to reflect where my life is today. Then I needed to create my purpose statement. My mission statement is my guide for how I want to live my life, and my purpose statement is why I want to live my life.

Current Mission Statement

"My God is the path I follow. My number one priority to care for and love is my family. My integrity makes me a creative individual always looking for

ways to be innovative in my life and career. My health and fitness give me strength to prepare for daily challenges. I will always share my talents and knowledge."

My Purpose Statement

"I help coach individuals and organizations ascend to their peak so they can achieve their dreams, goals, and ambitions."

As we continue on our journey through The High Achiever Leadership Formula, this chapter is the foundational component for you to become the leader you want to be. My hope is that this book helps you find the ingredients you need to become that inspiring and influential leader.

CHAPTER TAKEAWAYS

The High Achiever Mindset formula:
Energy + Connections + Influence + Integrations = Great Results

Mindset is a particular way of thinking; a person's attitude or set of opinions about something, a mental attitude or inclination; a fixed state of mind.

The **Climber Mindset** is searching to grow, learn, change, and become who you want to be. You are always finding new ways to accomplish goals and are willing to keep trying even when you fail. You realize your ascension in life is about continuing to grow each day.

The **Stuck Mindset** is never wanting to fail. You always stay on the safe path and are unwilling to grow, learn, or change. You talk about the past and why the future is never going to be any better.

High achievers look for ways to become more energized in these three areas:

Physical   Nutritional   Daily Boosts

The foundation for high-quality connection is based on three areas:

Cognitive   Emotional   Behavioral

Three-part plan to connect to those closest to you:
- Disconnect from technology and communicate face-to-face.
- Keep your breakfast and dinner table free from electronics.
- Don't multi-task when you are communicating.

2

The Leadership
Time Solution

"The key is not to prioritize what's on your schedule, but to schedule your priorities."

-Stephen Covey

I was driving into work one morning and listening to the news when the newscaster said something that grabbed my attention. "Scientists recently discovered that the twenty-four hour daily cycle really should be based on a twenty-five hour cycle." I snapped to attention and thought of all the things I could do with an extra hour each day such as exercise, spend more time with my family, sleep, read, meet with friends, spend an extra hour at the office, etc. As the news story continued, I realized I had taken what I heard out of context, but my initial response started to make me think: What would I really do with an extra hour each day which totaled seven in a week and thirty each month? That would add up to three hundred sixty-five hours in a year. That would be over nine forty-hour work weeks each year. What would I do with all that extra time? What would you do?

I realize we aren't really going to start having twenty-five-hour days, but I do believe that with the right system, process and framework in place, we can create an additional hour each day in our lives. The challenge we have is the willingness to change our current behaviors to implement new strategies which will make us more effective and efficient. Creating a new, disciplined behavior is about creating a framework to make each minute of the day count. The issue is not the lack of time but the lack of prioritization.

Over the years I have followed Stephen Covey's work in The 7 Habits of Highly Effective People (Covey, 1989). I have become a facilitator for this program along with his courses of "Focus" and "The 5 Choices." The key to each one of these is the realization that we don't manage time; we manage our priorities. I have reviewed some of the best strategies from multiple sources to create my own system called "The Leadership Time Solution," which is about creating a daily and weekly framework and strategies to prioritize what is most important. When we just allow our days to happen, we become unproductive, unorganized, and uninspired to do what needs to be accomplished.

As we continue, I challenge you to make some changes with the way you currently do your planning. You will likely resist the change and try to reason that it will not work. My pledge to you is that if you implement this framework and follow it for the next thirty days, you will be more productive, happy, and excited about your daily accomplishments. It will take willpower for you to succeed, but once you have expended the willpower to make it a standard operating procedure, it will become a relatively automatic mental process.

THE PROBLEM

The problem is not that we only have twenty-four hours in a day, but how productive we are in those twenty-four hours. Why does it seem some people get more accomplished in those hours than others? Time management is more than managing our time. It's about setting priorities and taking charge of your willpower. It means changing habits and behaviors that cause us to waste time.

We allow one day to look the same as another:

- Always thinking about work
- Strain between work and home
- Working harder with less is the new norm
- Continual sense of fatigue
- Constant "stuff" and "messes"
- Crisis driven
- Same as everyone else I work with
- Email overload

"The Leadership Time Solution" is a powerful way to focus your time, energy, creativity, and productivity in order to create better results and behaviors. It frees you so you can spend more time being an influential leader. In this day and age it's too easy to get caught in the trap of juggling countless activities each day. You have to protect your time with a system. Managing multiple tasks while knowing you have a major project to complete does not help complete the major project. Our system stresses you must decide your top three projects each week so that your business or personal goals move forward. If you don't, you will see that you are pulled in multiple time-wasting directions.

As you look at the picture, which box do you fit into? I was once very mechanical and reactive in my daily priorities. Even though I have studied, written, and trained others about this material, I still have days that I become very mechanical and reactive. I have realized the more planning and prioritizing I do, the less I become involved in the mechanical and reactive mode.

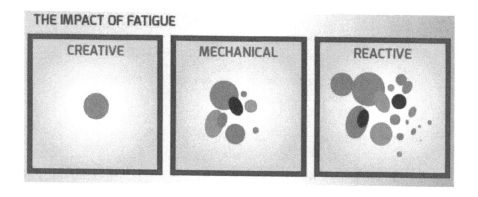

THE SOLUTION

Implementing "The Leadership Time Solution" through the PRO system allows greater Productivity, Recovery Time, and less Office Time each day. When you schedule your time and work your plan, you will see improved work-life balance. I am a father of three children, and it seems we are always running to a school activity, sports practice, or game. The challenge is not only my schedule but also the family schedule. I have realized that my children will only be these ages for a short time, and if I do not make it a priority to attend their activities, I will have allowed precious moments to slip by. The regret of missing them is summed up in Harry Chapin's song "Cats in the Cradle" (Harry Chapin, 1974). The song speaks of the regret we will all experience if we don't take the time to determine our priorities. We must create daily and weekly schedules if we don't want to wake up someday with the regret of missing the best part of our children's lives.

"The Leadership Time Solution" breaks your activities into the PRO System consisting of three distinct categories: Peak Productivity Time, Recovery Time, and Office Time. The following are some benefits of the PRO System:

- Increases recovery time thus increasing job performance
- Schedules your days and weeks
- Expands your interests outside of work
- Frees you from "stuff" and "messes"
- Adds physical and mental energy
- Promotes harmony between work and home
- Provides excitement when goals are achieved
- Intensifies loyalty
- Gives a greater purpose to life
- Evens work-life balance

Peak Productivity Time

Peak Productivity Time is the daily time that you do your planning and forward thinking. This time is the most valuable because it is focused on your revenue generating income or the most important projects of the week. This could be working with clients, determining sales strategy, improving systems and processes, making sales calls, or setting appointments with clients.

I suggest you schedule Peak Productivity Time in 90-minute segments and make this the highest priority on your calendar each day. Schedule, block your calendar, and explain to your staff why this is critical to you and the business. The concept of the 90-minutes came from <u>The Power of Full Engagement</u> by Loehr and Schwartz (Loehr and Schwartz, 2004). This rhythm is called BRAC (Basic Rest-Activity Cycle). In the 1970s further research showed that a version of the same 90-to-120 minute cycles, ultradian rhythms, help to account for the ebb and flow of our energy throughout the day. Physiological measures such as heart rate, hormonal levels, muscle tension, brain-wave activity, and alertness all increase during the first part of the cycle. After an hour or so these measures start to decline. Somewhere between 90 and 120 minutes the body begins to crave a period of rest and recovery. We must make Peak Productivity Time a priority to experience increased productivity and a surge in momentum which will lead to greater creativity in less time.

Some ground rules to follow:

- Focus on your top three weekly projects during Peak Productivity Time.
- Implement 90-minute Peak Productivity Time which is scheduled in advance.
- Use this time for planning and forward thinking.
- Don't trade or skip this time.
- Educate your staff about the importance of Peak Productivity Time.
- Make a 90-minute "No Distraction" sign.
- Use a timer when you are in Peak Productivity Time, and take a break every 90 minutes for rest and recovery.
- Refrain from wireless phone use and email during this time.

Recovery Time

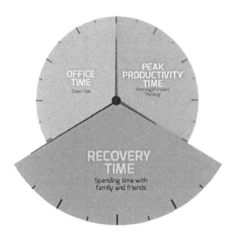

The PRO System makes you identify when you are going to have free time and builds a support system into your planning. In fact, it is necessary for periods of high achievement. Recovery Time allows you to come back with a new perspective and a better sense of direction. You will also find that you are more creative and full of fresh ideas and innovations. You will quickly find solutions to issues or problems helping you lead yourself and your team more efficiently. Recovery Time becomes a "must" versus a "should." The longer you go without Recovery Time, the more susceptible you will be to the daily grind and unable to handle even the routine activities efficiently. It becomes harder to implement new innovative approaches to solving daily problems. Eventually, you get into a "firefighting" mode in which everything becomes reactive and a crisis situation.

Some Recovery Time ground rules:

- Delegate and explain to staff how to handle issues while you are away.
- Do not focus on business-related thinking or reading.
- Avoid communication such as email, text messages, and notifications.
- Plan your activities for greater enjoyment and Recovery Time.
- Book vacations in advance.
- Schedule days off for Recovery Time.

Office Time

If used properly, Office Time can be one of the most valuable sessions you create for yourself. Too often we allow disorganized hours and days to get in the way of gaining a sense of progress and accomplishment of achieving our overall goals. Office Time allows you to prepare for your Peak Productivity Time. You must schedule and block this time just as you do with Peak Productivity Time and Recovery Time. Office Time is for taking care of the "stuff" and "messes" that are part of every day. It's when you delegate your work, go through emails and correspondence, and clean up the "stuff" that piled up during the day or week.

Some sample clean ups that when not identified will add to the frustration and complexity of our lives:

- Administrative details
- Bookkeeping/accounting
- Reviewing reports
- Research
- Email
- Scheduling
- Appointments
- Delegation of tasks
- Follow up with staff

If not scheduled in advance, your hours can run together and your days are constantly disrupted. Interruptions are allowed during this time.

Some ground rules to follow in Office Time:

- Prepare for Peak Productivity Time and Recovery Time.
- Clean up your "stuff" and "messes."
- Delegate assignments to your staff.
- Schedule staff meetings and updates.
- Acquire new skills/training.
- Review budgets and reports.
- Manage your inbox.
- Create "My Weekly Plan."
- Create your "Daily Dashboard."

"My Weekly Plan" and "Daily Dashboard" will be explained later.

It takes time to create and become effective in "The Leadership Time Solution," but the benefits for you, your family, and business outweighs any struggle of implementation. As I put these ground rules in place, I could and did accomplish the key projects and tasks I had scheduled each week. Accomplishing what is most important each day increases your personal satisfaction, and you gain momentum for the next day.

"Momentum is like a merry-go-round that starts very slowly. Based on our daily actions, the energy increases."

-Gary Wilbers

THE THREE STAGES

Creating a system for high achievement takes a disciplined effort in order to generate the necessary behaviors to make your time the most productive. Stop and think about that. First, you must have a system to follow. Then you must discipline yourself to follow the system before your behaviors change. Most people allow one day to lead into another without any real planning about how their days will evolve.

As I coach, train, and speak about "The High Achiever Mindset," I have found "The Leadership Time Solution" to be a valuable tool in helping others solve this issue. It instructs how to plan your day's activities for maximizing your productivity. Do you know anyone who doesn't want to be more productive? By understanding the process, you will better understand the importance of the three stages in "The Leadership Time Solution."

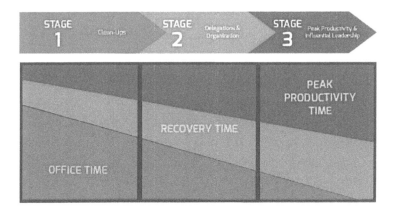

In this illustration there are three stages for implementing this system. The first stage is the Clean-Up Stage in which we spend more time in Office Time. In the second stage, the Delegation and Organization Stage, we increase our Peak Productivity Time and Recovery Time and reduce our Office Time. In the third stage we increase our Peak Productivity Time and Influential Leadership because we spend the majority of our time with our most important priorities. Remember: Implementing the system takes time. We recommend starting a habit by doing this for 90 days in order to implement the system into your daily habits and routines.

Stage 1 Clean Ups

This is where you are before implementing the system. Typically, very little of your day is spent in Recovery Time or Peak Productivity Time. Most of your day is spent in Office Time dealing with day-to-day problems which is why days seem so chaotic and hectic. You have no real organization except for what is on your calendar. You seem to have a lot to do, but you want and allow interruptions to rule each day. Your desk has multiple projects and papers so as to suggest you are busy and important, but in reality your organization has no purpose.

Stage 2 Delegations And Organization

In this stage you are implementing "The Leadership Time Solution" and beginning to experience some small wins in Recovery Time and Peak Productivity Time thus allowing you to rejuvenate and spend time with family and friends. Your Peak Productivity Time allows you to organize your most important projects and activities each week. As you learn to let your mind slow down and recover, you begin to feel more refreshed and ready to take on daily challenges. You start to control your days, set appointments, and use time blocking to complete your most important priorities.

Stage 3 Peak Productivity And Influential Leadership

In stage three you have begun mastery in utilizing the PRO system. You are accomplishing so much more in a shorter amount of time. You only do what is important and productive, eliminating time-wasting activities. The hours spent in Recovery Time allow you to clear your mind enabling you to easily solve problems and issues that arise. You have reached a level of Influential Leadership with others and your team by delegating tasks and holding them accountable for their results. In this stage Recovery Time increases and Office Time decreases. You are now working smarter.

THE IMPLEMENTATION PROCESS

The success of integrating any new system into your daily routine is creating practical tools that will help you with the process of implementation. In the final section of this chapter, I will be sharing and explaining some of the practical tools we have created to help you implement "The Leadership Time Solution" into your daily life. If we want to be more productive, we must hold ourselves accountable for taking the necessary steps to achieve that goal.

First, we must take an inventory of where we currently are in each area:

- Write three activities you want to increase in each area of the PRO system.
- Write a list of actions you need to implement in each area of the PRO System.

When you have completed these lists, it will help you understand and know which actions you need to start for successfully implementing your new system.

My Weekly Plan

The goal of creating "My Weekly Plan" is to review your schedule, plan your priorities for the week, and block your schedule for each area of the PRO system. It is important to realize that when you fill out "My Weekly Plan," you are filling it out for both your professional and personal roles. You must look at both areas in your weekly planning, or you will not be able to achieve the work-life balance you desire. This process should take less than thirty minutes each week and will give you a complete view of what is most important.

Top 3 Accomplishments Last Week	My Executive Dashboard		
	Project	Action This Week	✓
1	1		
2	2		
	3		
3	4		
	5		
Top 3 Projects This Week ✓	6		
1	7		
2	8		
	9		
3	10		
Positive Actions I Will Do For Others ✓	**My Teams Dashboard**		
	Name	Project / Task	✓
1			
2			

Past Accomplishments

At the top you see a place for your name, date, date you start for planning that week, and the end date. The first area to fill in is the "Top 3 Accomplishments Last Week." It is vital not to skip this area because this helps you to look back on your previous week and give yourself credit for good things that happened. We typically are very hard on ourselves, and it helps if we give ourselves a shot of dopamine, the body's natural chemical released in our brain when we experience joy. Using that joy helps us complete what we need to do this week.

Projects

The next area is the "Top 3 Projects This Week." Ask yourself: "What are the top three projects to complete or move forward?" If you are honest with yourself, you know you cannot complete more than three each week.

Positive Actions

The next section asks what "Positive Actions I Will Do For Others" this week. This area is about the most important people in your life, team, business, etc. Think of three people each week to whom you need to show some appreciation and gratitude. Purposely schedule time to make them feel special or appreciated. Remember: You become an influential leader by your actions.

Executive Dashboard

The "My Executive Dashboard" allows you to list out other projects and actions you need to take to keep moving things forward which helps you prioritize the calls and actions you need to complete this week. The challenge in this section is to put only the things you need to do **this** week since we receive a dopamine boost when we are able to check off completed items on our list.

Team's Dashboard

The last area is "My Team's Dashboard." This list is a quick reference of delegated items you need to check on, or items you may still need to assign. Use this list to help you organize the things you want to communicate to someone on your team.

My Weekly Plan

Top 3 Projects This Week

Time	Monday	Tuesday	Wednesday	Thursday	Friday	To Do List

Blocking Time

The back page of the "My Weekly Plan" is transferring over your top three projects for the week and then blocking your schedule to make sure you complete your highest priorities. I understand with electronic calendars this area may not be used, but it is a useful tool for deciding where to block 90-minute Peak Productivity Time, Office Time, or Recovery Time. I suggest you transfer this into your electronic calendar by color coding each area to make it stand out. For example, I use red for Peak Productivity Time, green for Recovery Time, and blue for Office Time. The last is a "To Do List" for items you think you might need to consider for next week or next month.

The key to "My Weekly Plan" is doing it each week. You can complete it first thing on Monday morning or the last thing on Friday afternoon. Don't plan on Sunday evening because this interrupts your Recovery Time. The key is to do it and plan to complete it each week.

Darren Hardy said in "Darren's Daily Message" ("Daily Mentoring for Achievers," n.d.) that Tuesday is the most productive day of the week followed by Wednesday. Realizing this, I changed my staff meetings to Monday and made changes on "My Weekly Plan" to complete my top three projects and priorities on these days.

Daily Dashboard

This practical tool is one that you should use every day to create Peak Productivity planning. It should only take five minutes or less to fill out, but it has lasting benefits for impacting your day. Have you ever heard the saying: "Lack of planning creates lack of completion."? This tool allows you to see your most important priorities each day. Reference your calendar to help you fill out your "Daily Dashboard." I suggest completing your "Daily Dashboard" at the end of each day or the first thing in the morning. The challenge is not to allow your email to rule your day. I suggest not checking your email until you have completed your first major priority.

Priorities

The first area to fill out in the "Daily Dashboard" is your "Priorities" for the day. The key is asking yourself this question: "No matter what, what must I complete today?" This list should be from one to five priorities. This is my biggest challenge because I want to list each item. For example, the day I started writing this chapter, I had five priorities listed. If I was really going to help move my major project forward, should I have listed five priorities? No, I

PEAK PRODUCTIVITY PLANNING

PRIORITIES What I Must Complete Today, No Matter What.

1
2
3
4
5

PEOPLE Who I Need to Reach Today.   Who I'm Waiting On.

PROJECTS Top 3 Projects for the Week.

1	2	3
Actions I must do this week to move this project forward.	Actions I must do this week to move this project forward.	Actions I must do this week to move this project forward.
A	A	A
B	B	B

should have only listed writing this chapter of my book. The other question is "What if I have more than five?" If they are truly priorities and you have more than five, you cannot expect to complete them. I notice on most days I can only complete one-to-three depending on the size of the priority. Set yourself up for success, not failure.

People

The middle section is for you to list the people you need to reach out to today. This can be by email or calling. If you are reaching out to clients, use whatever means they want to be communicated with. Understanding your client's preferences allows for the best communication. The second area provides a place for reminding you who you are waiting on for follow up.

Projects

The last area is for listing your "Top 3 Projects for the Week." This is transferred from your "My Weekly Plan." I suggest putting down the actions you must do this week for moving the project forward. Most of the time you will not be able to complete a major project in one week. This allows you to break it down into smaller increments. You have heard the saying, "How do you eat an elephant? One bite at a time." Make sure you put your "Top 3 Projects" on your "Daily Dashboard" every day of the week. This helps you to focus your attention later in the week on what you said was most important on Monday. If you skip this area, you will not move your major projects forward each week, and it becomes frustrating. This one simple tool can increase your productivity each day if you take the five minutes to complete.

The one challenge I hear when I present these practical tools is "Do I really need to write out 'My Weekly Plan' and 'My Daily Dashboard'?" In Focus: The Hidden Driver of Excellence, Daniel Goleman (Goleman and Goleman, 2013) explains that Self–awareness, mainly accuracy in decrypting the internal cues of our body's murmurs, is crucial. Our subtle physiological reactions mirror the sum total of our experience pertinent to the decision at hand. So if you really want to improve your productivity both personally and professionally, you need to write out your plan and then take the action to complete it. <u>The Attention Economy</u>, (Davenport and Beck, 2001) explains that human attention is extremely low so understanding and managing it is now the most essential factor of business success.

Habit Maker

Since we know it is hard to implement change in our lives regardless of how positive it may be, I developed a simple form called "The Habit Maker" to help myself develop and solidify new habits. Normally we give up before generating success.

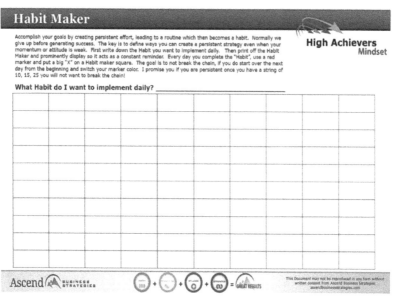

The key is to define ways you can create a persistent strategy even when your momentum is weak. First, write the habit you want to implement daily. Then print off "The Habit Maker" and prominently display it as a constant reminder. Every day you complete the habit successfully, use a red marker to put a big "X" on that square. The goal is not to break the chain. If you do, start over the next day and switch your marker color. It takes at least twenty-one days to form a new habit. That's why you have to start over if you miss a day. Consistency ingrains a new action into our routine.

"The Habit Maker" is a practice I used to write this book. The hardest part I had each day was getting started, but once I had a streak of ten days in a row, I did not want to break the chain. I recommend you try it for any habit you are wanting to implement into your life. You already know the most successful people do the things other people don't want to. The reason they are successful is because they are persistent.

SUMMARY

"The Leadership Time Solution" is a productivity tool that benefits your life both personally and professionally. When we began this chapter, I talked about what you would do if you had an extra hour each day. By putting a system in place, you cannot only have your extra hour but also be successful. Do not expect this to happen quickly. It takes time to implement and make the necessary behavioral changes. I have been studying time management for the last twenty-five years, and I still need to take daily and weekly action to be successful. Do I fail at times? Yes, but the one constant is I have a framework and system to follow each day, week, month, and year.

Self-esteem will help you achieve this goal. John Tierney and Roy Baumeister, authors of Willpower, (Baumeister and Tierney, 2011) explain there are two clearly demonstrated benefits of high self-esteem: 1) It increases initiative because it leads to confidence.

People with high self-esteem are more willing to act on their belief, stand up for what they believe, approach others, and risk new undertakings. 2) It feels good. High self-esteem seems to operate like a bank of positive emotions, which furnish a general sense of well-being and can be useful when you need an extra dose of confidence to cope with misfortune, ward off depression, or recover from failure.

If you have high self-esteem, you will be more likely to not only implement "The Leadership Time Solution" but also continue to make it a behavior that becomes a habit. It's not what we read that matters; it is what we implement that makes the greatest difference.

"Time Management is not about managing time but what you do with your time."

-Gary Wilbers

CHAPTER TAKEAWAYS

Time Management is more than managing our time. It's about setting priorities and taking charge of your willpower.

"The Leadership Time Solution" is a powerful way to focus your time, energy, creativity, and productivity to create better results and behaviors. It breaks your activities into The PRO System: Peak Productivity Time for daily planning, Recovery Time for allowing you to come back with a new perspective and better sense of direction, and Office Time for taking care of the everyday "stuff" and "messes."

How days evolve

- Clean ups
  - Where you are before implementing the system
- Delegations and Organization
  - Start the process of implementing "The Leadership Time Solution" and begin to experience some small wins in Recovery Time and Peak Productivity Time
- Peak Productivity and Influential Leadership
  - Started mastery in utilizing The PRO System

"My Weekly Plan" is for reviewing your schedule, planning your priorities, and blocking your schedule for each area of The PRO System.

"The Daily Dashboard" is for creating Peak Productivity planning.

"The Habit Maker" is for helping you accomplish your goals by creating a persistent effort leading to a routine which then becomes a habit.

3

The Leadership Communication Loop

"Communication is a skill that you can learn. It's like riding a bicycle or typing. If you're willing to work at it, you can rapidly improve the quality of every part of your life."

-Brian Tracy

Have you ever been sharing with one of your employees and wonder why you're getting that deer-in-the-headlights look? Did he/she even understand what you were saying? Perhaps the problem is the way YOU are communicating.

I remember early in my years as an entrepreneur, I thought I had all the answers and was looking for employees who would follow directions and do as I said. I look back now and realize what a mistake I made in leading them. Today our employees want to be engaged in something bigger than themselves. How we use our communication determines if the employee will decide to stay on our team or find a new one. Our communication strategy will establish if we are in business in the next ten years. I vividly remember one time when I was sharing with one of my employees something that needed to be completed. She gave me an expression which indicated she was not going to do that. I took my hand, slammed it on the desk, and said, "This is how it needs to be done, and you will do it!" This was totally wrong, but I did not understand what I now know about communication. That employee and I now laugh about that incident because over the years I have dramatically changed my demanding communication style to one of collaboration. In this chapter we are going to explore The Leadership Communication Loop which will help implement a strategy for communication in both your workplace and personal life.

Communication, the bedrock of modern civilization, has evolved dramatically over the last century. There seems to be every form imaginable, which should be a good thing. However, every day we see differently. As communication forms have evolved, our ability to effectively communicate has gradually diminished. So much that common workplace communication has become a struggle ending in confusion and confrontation.

COMMUNICATION

We have become a society which is moving further away from face-to-face communication and relying more on various other forms of technology. While some would say that shows we are progressing, it also shows that human interaction is fading. Nothing is as impacting and effective as face-to-face interactions when you are needing to influence change and performance directions.

One of the largest issues we have come across in the workplace over the years is the disconnection between management and employees about the topic of communication within the organization. Many times management feels communication is done well while the employees do not. Why is there such a gap between how the two areas of an organization see things? What we are seeing is a common situation which develops when one person communicates with another person based on how he/she would like to give and receive interaction. Rarely will that be effective because every person communicates in his/her own unique way. The truly effective communicator realizes this and "flexes" himself/herself so he/she can successfully relate to the other person. This allows an organization to efficiently and quickly move forward as well as minimize chances of conflict.

What do you think are the biggest barriers to successful communication strategies being implemented in an organization? Time? Money? Follow-up? While all of these are important and do have some impact, the largest obstacles are getting management and owners to understand there is a need and how important successful and effective communication truly is. Siemens Enterprise Communications (Technologies, 2016) estimates a business with 100 employees spends an average downtime of 17 hours a week clarifying communications translating to an average annual cost of $528,443. A SMB Communications (SMB Communications Study: Uncovering Costs of Communications Barriers And Latency, 2010) study showed that in January 2009 the cumulative cost per worker per year due to productivity losses resulting from communication barriers equaled $26, 041. Common sense tells us that if the communication barriers stayed the same or lessened a bit, the cost of labor will continue to increase. We need to get communication right.

It is important to realize that as we communicate we generally have a thought or image in mind of what we wish to convey. The problem occurs because the one talking knows the image or message, but the person listening doesn't. For example, if I told you I had just purchased a pretty blue Chevy, we could easily have two very different visualizations of that car. If that were the end of our conversation, I could think I gave the message clearly. However, you may have an entirely different image in your mind.

This situation frequently arises in the workplace as there are messages going back and forth in a very hurried and often stressful environment. Complicating matters is the fact that we are living during a time period where as many as four generations are working in the same place and doing the same jobs simultaneously. That alone leads to many communication issues undermining the overall efficiency of any organization. Adding poor communication into the mix, profit and productivity will NEVER reach full potential, nor will the culture of the organization ever become one that has a climber mindset behind it.

Some will say it is the duty of the employees to make sure they understand the leader, and the leader's job is to put the message out there for the team.

"Developing excellent communication skills is absolutely essential to effective leadership. The leader must be able to share knowledge and ideas to transmit a sense of urgency and enthusiasm to others. If a leader can't get a message across clearly and motivate others to act on it, then having a message doesn't even matter."

-Gilbert Amelio, President and CEO of National Semiconductor Corp.

This quote acknowledges that it is imperative for a leader or anyone who is trying to get a message across to know how to communicate well and make his/her message meaningful. Clarity of the message and understanding your audience are paramount to making sure you accomplish what you set out to do.

GENERATIONAL COMMUNICATION

As we begin our journey through the topic of effective communication, let's first look at how generations interact in communication.

Have you ever said to yourself, "I just don't understand people."? There is a real reason you feel this way, and it can be fixed. Currently, we face a situation relatively new in the workplace which presents a major hurdle for each of us. What is this issue? Generational differences. Each generation contains factors that have made us uniquely who we are, how we communicate and interact with others, and how we use that communication to better society. Without the proper understanding of these differences, we can never enjoy and leverage all the positive attributes each distinct generation offers.

You have to work on effective communication; otherwise, conflict will arise as different generations progress through situations. Because generational communication is on different levels, problems escalate needlessly. As this communication gap widens, it leads to decreased productivity, quality, and innovation. Unsolved generational differences develop into misunderstood attitudes and relationships and negatively impact the working environment. Less engaged employees lower motivation and initiative which damages teamwork.

How do we change that? Even though there are many things to consider when working with various generations, there are some basic principles you can use:

- Appreciate the differences.
- Acknowledge your interdependence.

- Appreciate what each generation does differently.
- Discover what things you have in common.
- Take on the responsibility to make a peaceful co-existence.

As we look at these different generations, a vast world of experience and knowledge opens up leading to a greater future for everyone. As we begin to understand how each generation communicates, we can actually build a stronger and more diverse workplace where we are working together and not against each other.

Each group has their basic traits and unique influencing factors. Looking at each group, think about the people you know who fall into these categories. See if you can identify some similar traits they display in their everyday life.

Traditionalists 1901-1943

- Follow chain of command
- Do not challenge authority
- Duty before pleasure
- Slow to change

Baby Boomers 1944-1964

- Challenge the status quo
- Question authority
- Competitive but fair
- Workaholic

Generation Xers 1965-1981

- Prefer email to the phone
- Ask why

- Greater work-life balance
- Want structure and direction

Millennials 1982-2003

- Raised with positive reinforcement
- Informal and good at multitasking
- Realistic
- Goal oriented
- Tolerant

It is important to realize why people are the way they are in order to more aptly communicate with them. Obviously, each generation will view things differently, but that doesn't mean they cannot co-exist in a workplace. In fact, each generation brings with them an array of skills and viewpoints that can enable a workplace to be very well-rounded.

Traditionalists

The Traditionalists are very stable employees who are practical and respectful. They will generally sacrifice themselves for the job and will need some help in navigating a work/life balance as they will have a tendency to work too much.

Baby Boomers

The Boomers are very service-oriented team players who generally have an optimistic outlook and a love/hate relationship with leadership. They are in the job for personal gratification which drives them to succeed. Boomers are open to integration of skills in the workplace.

Generation Xers

The Generation Xers are highly adaptable and technologically literate. They tend to have a skeptical outlook on life, and authority has to prove themselves to them. Though they are reluctant to commit, once they do, they are fully invested.

Millennials

The Millennials are great multi-taskers and tech-savvy. This group approaches work with a hopeful outlook and is polite to authority. Since this group was raised in the participation world, they are team-oriented. They fully embrace and encourage feedback.

If you had a group of employees that were fairly evenly distributed from the above generations, your organization could definitely be strong in many areas. The problem comes in when a particular generation views another as dispensable, too rigid, too loose, etc. The leaders need to actively encourage diversity and open communication among team members.

There are some basic principles that can be shared with each generation to help them when dealing with other generations which will ensure greater acceptance and ease of communication. A leader has the responsibility to teach the following things to each team member:

- Acceptance
- Interdependence
- Common ground
- Respect

Having various generations in one workplace setting does not have to be a stressful situation, but it does take a purposeful effort upon the part of management to ensure that each group is maximized and appreciated.

EIGHT PILLARS OF COMMUNICATION

In all things there has to be some basic principles. If you are building a house, you have to have a firm foundation. When beginning to start a business, you need a well-thought out business plan. It is no different when you consider communicating with people. You have to understand the basic principles if you wish to be successful.

Eight Pillars of Communication to consider when you are trying to communicate with those around you, especially if you feel you are struggling to get your message across:

Precision

It has been shown that we have difficulty concentrating on more than three-to-five things at once. Knowing that we often have to process various messages as well as do our job, it is important for clear and concise communication.

- Use personal names instead of pronouns.
- Use dates when possible.
- Utilize stories and real-life examples.
- Provide links or copy and paste what you are referencing.
- Get to the point quickly, politely, and specifically.

Connections

It is imperative that you make a connection with the people to whom you are speaking. It is also important that you quickly make a connection between them and the resolution to the current issue. When you can accomplish this, your message and action plan advances much faster than not making a direct correlation between the people and the solution.

- State the problem/issue quickly.
- Bring it to their level for a fast connection.
- Utilize motivating, encouraging power words:
  - Immediately, follow-up, accelerate, breakthrough, impact, etc.
- Use brief messages.
- Find and promote common ground.

Packaged

Keeping a message packaged means making sure you know your desired end result and then giving the pertinent information.

- Stay on topic.
- State your end result clearly.
- Bring the listener back to the topic if he/she begins to drift.
- Mention your topic more than once to ensure everyone gets the point you are trying to make.
- Recap the most important points in your message.

Clear

The clearness or clarity of the communication is critical to its overall success. Too often we communicate with ambiguity and then wonder why it is that our results do not resemble what we had planned. In today's workplace clear messages are the key to success.

- Identify the best channel or method for delivering your communication.
- Know your listener and pattern the communication accordingly.
- Keep it simple making sure you cover the needed items.
- Check for understanding by asking the listener to restate the principle message you conveyed.
- Stay in touch through follow-up and remain open-minded to questions.

Empathy

Many times when we communicate with others, we elicit some form of a response. This can take many forms from agreement to disagreement or excuses. A leader has to understand how to react to these with empathy and not sympathy. Empathy is an understanding of the communicator's feelings while encouraging him/her to continue trying. Sympathy is an understanding that causes one to indulge the other person often allowing him/her to underachieve.

- Put aside your own viewpoint and listen.
- Examine your attitude before speaking.
- Listen without distraction to hear what the other person is truly saying.
- Validate the other person's thoughts.
- Help the person discover answers to his/her issue.

Transparency

Many leaders struggle with this trait in their business. The leader feels that if he/she gives too much information, control will be lost. This is a BIG issue. The best path to take with any communication is to be completely transparent. Knowing there will always be some business proprietary issues that can't be shared, be as open as possible to enhance agreement on all projects.

- Respond with open and genuine positivity.
- Don't hide information from the team; the more informed, the better they will perform.
- Remain open to questioning; if you don't know the answer, tell them you will find it.
- Explain yourself and your decision.
- Accept feedback.
- Give positive feedback.

Fact-based

Outside of offending someone one of the worst things that can happen is to communicate on assumptions and not facts. Making sure you have all of your facts from trusted sources prior to communicating will help you make a positive, growing culture within your organization.

Respect

If people feel disrespected, they will not put forth their best efforts keeping your business from reaching its full potential.

- Don't interrupt, even if you know he/she is wrong.
- Listen and don't try to think of your response while he/she is talking.
- Listen with your heart and ears in order to determine what the true message is.
- Use positive words and phrases to encourage.
- Show appreciation in each interaction.

COMMUNICATION BARRIERS

The above Eight Pillars of Communication will help you break down these barriers to communication:

Environmental

Some barriers are due to the existing environment. For example, if you are standing in adverse weather conditions, your conversation would be hampered because you would not be able to pay full attention to what the other person is saying. Avoid distractions.

Distance

Distance also plays an important part in determining the course of a conversation. For example, if the staff in an organization are in different buildings or floors, they might have to substitute face-to-face communication with phone calls or emails.

Mode of Communication

Communication also includes using signs and symbols to convey a feeling or thought. However, if there is an ignorance about the medium you use to send the message, the conversation can be hindered.

Generational

Each age group has a different general approach to work. This often leads to conflicts because older workers describe younger workers as "slackers," and younger workers criticize older workers as "out of touch."

Status and Resistance

Workers accustomed to workplaces that emphasize seniority and status may find it difficult to adapt to more fluid environments where job titles are de-emphasized and production methods do not always follow a predetermined set of guidelines.

Geographical

Always consider the current location of the receiver. In our world of remote employees and global organizations, it is vital to the end result that you factor in how you will reach out to these employees and what back-up or follow-up you will do to ensure your message receives action.

Interpersonal

Desire to Participate

The lack of desire to participate in the communication process is a significant barrier. There is nothing more frustrating than trying to communicate with an individual that clearly does not want to.

Desire to Explore

Unwillingness to explore different ideas, opinions, and priorities creates communication barriers every day of our lives. This can be extremely frustrating.

Perceptual Barriers

Perceptual Filters

We all have our own preferences, values, attitudes, origins and life experiences that act as "filters" with our experiences of people, events, and information. Seeing things through the lens of our own unique life experiences or "conditioning" may lead to assumptions, stereotyping, and misunderstandings of others whose experiences differ from our own.

Triggers and Cues

What we say is affected by how we say it (tone, volume) and by our nonverbal cues (body language, facial gestures).

Emotional Barriers

Anger

This can affect the way your brain processes information.

Pride

The need to be right all the time will not only annoy others but also may shut down effective communication.

Anxiousness

Anxiety has a negative impact on the part of your brain that manages creativity and communication skills.

Probably the easiest way to ensure communication is happening the way it should is for the leader to fully listen to his/her people. It sounds simple, but do you realize a great deal of time was spent teaching you how to read, write, add, and subtract? However, very little time was invested in teaching you how to listen. As a matter of fact, recent studies (Begelow and Poremba, 2014) have shown that after the first day we hear something, we only retain about 85%. A month later it reduces to a maximum of 65%.

ACTIVE LISTENING

A way to combat this loss of content is by employing active listening, a way of listening which causes a person to often hear messages that generally are missed by the majority of people. Active Listening has five basic ingredients to help the listener assimilate all that is being said and retain it longer:

- No Distractions
- Body Language
- Clarity
- No Evaluating
- Respectful Response

Distractions

Having no distractions is crucial to better understanding and quicker, more complete responses. Here are some tips:

- Focus attention on the speaker.
- Maintain eye contact.
- Ignore potential distractions.
- Justify one conversation at a time when in groups of people.

Body Language

Body language is a tricky thing. Unbeknown to us often times we are displaying "negative" type body language. It takes a conscious effort to make sure we are giving the right message through our body language. Consider these tips:

- Make sure your gestures show openness.
- Nod occasionally.
- Be aware of your facial expressions.
- Avoid shifting back and forth as it gives the impression you are weary of the conversation.
- Use affirming comments for encouraging the speaker.

Clarity

Nothing can replace the clarity of a message which makes sure all involved parties understand exactly what is expected from them individually. That along with everyone knowing the time-frame for the task or issue to be resolved is paramount for success and optimized productivity. Here are some ways for increasing clarity:

- Occasionally paraphrase what is being said.
- Ask questions to gain clarity of the purpose, emotion, and intent.
- Summarize what has been said and ask if you have the correct interpretation.

Evaluating

The next ingredient to active listening is often times the hardest one to train our minds to do. When listening to someone, do not mentally evaluate even though you may not agree with his/her ideas. However, in a workplace these things must be put aside for work to be done and communication to happen flawlessly.

Here are some tips:

- Stay focused on what is being said and avoid trying to evaluate right or wrong.
- Even if you feel strongly about what is being said, allow the speaker to finish.
- Do not form your reply while the speaker is talking.
- Give your undivided attention to what is being said in order to not miss important details.

Respect

Finally, a respectful response is always called for regardless of the setting or who is involved. Not all the time will you agree with what is being said, but you should always reply in a very respectful manner. Here are some tips:

- Shield your honest response with respect for the speaker's viewpoint and feelings.
- Realize both you and the other person have opinions.
- Remember to give the same respect as you would like given to you.

Active listening is a vital trait to develop as a leader in today's fast-paced business environment. While many think it takes much too long to do this, the opposite is actually true. When you make a point to focus on the key issues, listen to what is being said and respond respectfully and clearly. Time is actually saved because there is no confusion or repeating.

Always remember to practice active listening as part of your conversation, and then utilize a three–step process to close the conversation:

- Paraphrase: Restate what you heard in your own words.
- Summarize: Gather the speaker's main points and repeat them for clarity.
- Questions: Ask questions to clarify both sides of the issue in order to ensure you both clearly understand.

WRITTEN COMMUNICATION

It seems as we move into a more tech-savvy world that certain arenas of communication are incurring great levels of misunderstanding. The one area suffering most is written communication. It seems more and more we are leaving communication's face-to-face origin and moving towards emails, texts, and chats. While these advancements have helped in many ways, they also have brought some issues. We have a large segment of society that communicates using emojis, texts without vowels, etc. Think about how many times you have received a text or email in ALL CAPS? What did you think when you saw that? How did it make you feel? Often the intentions of the sender and the receiver's interpretation are very different.

Not long ago I had an employee that responded to nearly everything in ALL CAPS and would put an exclamation mark at the end of every email. It was pretty confusing trying to decide if he was upset, happy, excited, or frustrated. The worst part was when he would not use all caps because that added an additional layer of confusion since it was out of his norm. Was he annoyed, didn't care what he replied, or in a hurry?

Email

It can be frustrating trying to interpret what others are trying to communicate. When you add a poorly communicated message, it further confuses the situation. Below you will find some tips to use when writing emails and writing in general communications:

Use Subject Lines as Headlines

Write a subject that grabs the reader's attention.

Write One Point per Email

If you need to communicate with someone about a number of different things, consider writing a separate email for each subject.

Specify the Response You Want

Include any preferred actions.

Utilize End of Message Headlines

You can put all the relevant information in the subject line followed by the letters "EOM" thus the subject line is the message.

Internal Email

- Do not be too informal.
- Always use your spell checker and avoid slang.
- Avoid overusing all capital letters.
- Only use capitalization for the important words.

Write For Success

When you are communicating through written words other than emails or texts, there is a wonderful model AIDA (Attention-Interest-Desire-Action) that dates back to the late 1800s and is attributed to Elias St. Elmo Lewis, an American advertising and sales pioneer. AIDA (Boundless, 2016) stresses that every kind of writing should be written for the purpose of capturing the reader's attention. Regardless of the mode of written communication, you always want to write for success. All writing should move a person to action. The four parts of AIDA blend together and make a perfect model for written communication:

Attention

Grab attention immediately by utilizing powerful wording or graphics in order to catch the reader's eye and make them stop and read. This should be short, powerful, and connecting to your audience. Always rethink your first paragraph and/or headline to ensure it captures your audience.

Interest

Gaining the reader's interest is a deep process. Use outlines, bullets, or other creative ways to cause the reader to see your message and become interested. Utilizing words that draw images in the reader's mind is also a powerful tool.

Desire

If you use the Interest section properly, it will lead directly to inspiring the reader's desire. The main way of doing this is by appealing to the reader's personal needs and wants. Wording things to pique the reader's desire is crucial to drawing action from him/her.

Action

No matter how interested a person is in what you have

written if you do not include a call to action, you will not get the desired results. The call to action has to be clear, specific, and time bound in order to move people. If you leave it vague or open-ended, people will tend to procrastinate.

Nothing is more important in the business world than having effective communication. A recent ExploreHR.org (Antariksa, n.d.) study showed that 70% of mistakes made in the workplace are a result of poor communication. Businesses today cannot afford to have preventable mistakes happening in their day-to-day operations. Effective communication will alleviate many issues and increase the overall culture of your organization to one of peak productivity and profitability.

CHAPTER TAKEAWAYS

Effective Communication is the bedrock of all healthy organizations and leaders.

A leader has the responsibility to teach the following things to each team member:

- Acceptance
- Interdependence
- Common ground
- Respect

When communicating in any form, remember these principles:

- Precision
- Connections
- Packaged
- Clear
- Empathy
- Transparency
- Fact-based
- Respect

When writing emails, practice the following:

- Use subject lines as headlines.
- Write one point per email.
- Specify the response you want.
- Utilize end of message headlines.
- Avoid using all capitalization.

Remember AIDA:

- Attention
- Interest
- Desire
- Action

4

The Influence and Trust Builder

"Leadership is not taken, it is given. People give leadership to those that they trust. They allow people that they trust to have influence over their lives."

-Henry Cloud

One of the most important things we can do in life is to leave a positive legacy. When do we start? Right Now. Whether you are a leader within an organization or leading your family through life, leaving a positive legacy will require you to understand two things: trust and influence. In this chapter we will explore how to take the essential steps to ensure that those you impact with your leadership are always getting your very best.

TRUST

When people allow you to be an influence in their lives, it is a bestowed privilege because you have earned it through a purposeful approach of placing others before yourself. You are trusted to the degree that people believe in your ability, consistency, integrity, and commitment to deliver. Trust is the competitive advantage gained when others confidently believe in you.

While it may appear to be static, in reality trust is more like a forest — a long time growing but easily burned down. It requires time, effort, diligence, and character. Inspiring trust is not easy to fake.

There are two dimensions of trust: time (short-to-long) and depth (shallow-to-deep). Deep trust, called transferred trust, is generally established over time and develops if a trusted source testifies you are trustworthy.

When trust is deeply established, you will often be given the benefit of the doubt instead of having every action skeptically judged. It gives a concrete, critical advantage and is the currency of business and life. In a climate of trust, people are more creative, motivated, productive, and willing to sacrifice for the team. It is essential when trying to live a life of influence.

INFLUENCE

Some people have lots of influence on those with whom they interact while others have very little. Why is that? It comes from the difference between influence and persuasion. Persuasion, a form of influence, is used as needed; influence is who you are.

We should never forget that influence is always active. You are either negatively or positively influencing someone all the time. Those who have very little positive influence over those they lead have four general traits preventing them from having a long-lasting positive influence:

- They neglect building relationships based on the other person's good.
- They disconnect from those around them unless they want something.
- They are concerned with self and self-gain and have little room for anyone else.
- Their decisions are perceived as inconsistent.

People who struggle gaining positive influence with others will almost always display some or all of the above four traits. The main reason is because somewhere along the way they missed the most prevalent concept of learning and behavior modification: To learn and grow you must be purposeful. It will never just happen by itself.

Let me share a story to explain influence:

Monday, March 10, 2014, my phone rang and my golf partner Keith told me his dad had passed away the night before. His father had been sick, but I hadn't realized the gravity. I reassured Keith telling him everything would be okay, and I was praying for him and his family. Keith and I share a special bond. We have been Unified Golf partners with Special Olympics Missouri for the past seven years. Unified Golf features nine holes with teams consisting of one athlete and one partner.

My friend Keith was diagnosed with down-syndrome shortly after birth. Even though we grew up in the same town, I didn't know Keith personally, but I attended school with his sister so I knew about him. I learned Keith was outgoing and energetic in spite of his challenges. I became acquainted with Keith on a personal level when I became involved in Special Olympics. One Sunday after Mass, he asked me if I would be his Unified Golf partner. I was honored but quickly explained that I was not a very good golfer. Keith assured me he could "show me the ropes," and we would just do our best and everything would be ok.

In 2010, Keith and I had the honor of representing Missouri Special Olympics at the National Games in Lincoln, Nebraska. The experience will remain with me forever. Athletes all across the United States were competing for nothing more than to do their best. Keith and I were going into our last round with a chance for the gold, but our quest was denied by one stroke.

As I drove to the visitation for Keith's dad Lawrence, I prayed for the right words to say. I knew Keith's dad was his hero. Over the last seven years his dad would bring him to practice, and if I was not able to make it, he would fill in for me. Going through the line, I gave Keith a big hug and said I was praying for him. Keith responded, "Gary, I am going to miss my dad." I told him, "I will too." Lawrence was a kind, gentle giant and an important role model for me. We would often discuss life, and over the years he showed me how to treat my family and how to truly live. He always thanked me for what I did for Keith, but in reality, I should have been thanking him.

A month later Keith caught me after church and asked if I was ready to start playing golf again and win a gold medal. I wasn't surprised because every year Keith wanted to win the gold medal. As always I said we would give it our best shot. Keith responded back, "No, Gary, you don't understand. I want to win the gold medal this year for my dad." WOW! I felt as though he had just placed a ton of bricks on my back. In May Keith and I started weekly practices. Knowing how much it meant to Keith, I had my best attendance at practice that year. Every practice Keith reminded me why he wanted to win the gold, and I always responded we have to do our best and leave the rest in God's hands.

The day of our Regional tournament, I was closing out a business and moving furniture and fixtures. I finished around three o'clock and headed straight to the course. I remember getting into my vehicle and feeling extremely tired. As I was driving, I thought about Keith's goal of winning the gold medal. I was exhausted and did not feel like playing golf. I said a prayer asking God to be with us. I knew I needed his help. My thoughts went back to Keith, his dad, and our times together on the course. I asked Lawrence to be our special angel that day.

As I arrived at the course, Keith was very excited to get started. He kept saying, "We got to win the gold for my dad today." I started getting nervous and anxious because I have never been the greatest golfer. To help settle me, I asked Keith to join me in prayer. We prayed for his dad and for us to have a good round of golf, and if God was willing, for us to win the gold medal. After our first three holes, I could tell Keith was nervous and not playing his regular game. I asked him what was wrong. With tears in his eyes, he replied, "I want to win so badly for my dad." I told Keith, "Let's just have fun, play for your dad, and let God take care of the rest." Keith surprised me by settling in and playing his A-game. I was actually playing a pretty good round myself. It turned out that being tired slowed my swing, and my shots were much straighter. After six holes we had a good score, but we did not know how our competition was doing.

Our next hole was a par three across water. I was tense because previously on this very hole I have hit my ball into the water. I retrieved my eight iron, swung, and my ball landed right in the middle of the green. Keith and I made par on the hole. Eventually, we came in with a score of forty-seven. It was one of the best rounds we had ever played. I felt good and hoped it would be enough to achieve Keith's goal of a gold medal.

As we lined up for the awards presentation, we were stationed in the middle of two other teams. I knew this meant we had won the gold, but Keith didn't. He kept asking, "Gary, did we win the gold?" I just shrugged and told him we would have to wait and see. We clapped as they announced the bronze and silver medalists. Then they were announcing our names as the gold medalist winners. I will never forget this moment. Keith looked up to the sky and said, "Dad, that was for you." Then he made the Sign of the Cross. With tears rolling down my cheeks, I silently thanked God for allowing Keith this opportunity.

Keith's family had watched and came to congratulate us. As we all shared hugs, Keith said, "Gary, now we get to go to State. Isn't that great?" I responded, "Yes, that will be great, Keith." Keith then responded, "Now, we have to win the gold medal at State for my dad." I took a deep breath, smiled, and said, "We will give it our best shot, Partner."

The next month and a half we continued practicing for State. Every practice Keith would talk about winning gold for his dad. That year State was held in our home town. A couple of days before the tournament, I received a call from a local TV station reporter asking about our quest for gold. He told me he had heard about it from the Public Relations Manager at Missouri Special Olympics. I told him the story about Keith playing for gold to honor his father who had passed away in March. The reporter wanted to join us on the course and take some footage for a story about Keith.

The morning of the tournament was a dreary, cold, windy day with thunderstorms. As I arrived at the course, Keith was ready to get started. The reporter introduced himself and asked if he could interview Keith and me and take some footage on the course. Keith was so excited. He told everyone he was going to be on TV.

We began our warm up, and I kept telling myself to relax. I was nervous and anxious because I wanted Keith to achieve his dream. At the first tee, Keith and I said a quick prayer. Keith wanted the first shot so he started us off. The ball went less than 50 yards, and he came back to the cart very upset. I said, "Just relax and let's have fun." Over the years that has been my motto because when either one of us gets too serious, we don't play very well. We recovered from that challenge and had headed to the second hole when it started to drizzle. After our first three holes, we were not playing very well. We scored seven on the first hole, six on the second, and seven on the third. Keith continually asked the score, and I kept telling him, "Let's not worry about the score. Let's just play golf and have fun."

I realized during those first three holes the reporter was making us nervous, so I told Keith to pretend he was not there and that we were just playing a practice round and having fun. It worked. On the next two holes, we scored a four and six. As we approached our sixth hole, the rain and wind picked up. Keith and I had a really bad hole and scored a ten, the highest score you are allowed to have in Unified Golf. We were so frustrated. Again, I told Keith not to worry about that hole and suggested we finish strong on the last three.

As we approached the seventh hole, rain started to pour and lightning flashed across the sky. The air horn blew telling us to stop playing and return to the clubhouse. Driving to the clubhouse, I was thinking we didn't have a chance for the gold medal. We waited on the rain to subside, but when it didn't, the officials decided to use the scores from the six holes played to determine the winners. Keith asked, "Do you think we won gold?" I tried to be positive and responded, "You never know."

As they started preparation for the awards, the reporter and I were talking. He mentioned how great it would be if we were to win the gold. I confided to him that I did not think it was possible.

They called our division to the front which was crowded with golfers, parents, and volunteers. We huddled around the officials. There was no line-up as in previous tournaments which suggested who the winners were. Officials announced the bronze medalists. I was somewhat surprised it was not us. Then came the silver medalists, and it was not us either. Finally, it was time for the gold. The official announced, "The gold medal goes to Keith Lueckenoff playing today in memory of his dad with partner Gary Wilbers." We had done it. We received our medals, and with tears streaming down his face, Keith gave me the biggest hug and said, "Gary, I think my dad is proud of me." I told Keith, "I think your dad was our guardian angel today." Keith's family came to congratulate us, and I silently said a prayer thanking God for this moment.

Our quest for gold was completed because one of God's angels made a request to let one of his earthly angels shine brightly that day.

This story shows the influence and impact Keith and his dad have had in my life. Many people tell me how nice it is that I play golf with Keith. They are missing the point: Keith is actually the one influencing me because he continually shows me how to enjoy life through every difficulty or challenge. Keith has inspired me to place others before myself.

PERSUASION

Persuasion is utilized more as a negotiation technique. It is a temporary framework allowing you to achieve a certain goal in a moment of time. If handled correctly, these six crucial parts will allow you to be successful in any bargaining or negotiating situation:

Be Respectful

Often times when two or more parties come to a point of negotiation, one or the other becomes defensive. In order to be successful in this situation, you must realize that the other person and his/her views are valuable and needed in order to make progress towards an advantageous agreement.

Deliver A Specific Benefit

If you only look at a situation from your point of view, you will never be able to deliver the benefit the other party is looking for in order to reach an agreement. You will need to discover what is most important to the other person in order for you to be successful.

Define The Impact

When you are trying to persuade someone towards a new way of thinking, you have to show him/her why **NOT** subscribing to your way of thinking will have a negative impact on his/her work or personal life. Even though you do not want to dwell on the negative, it is important to realize that many people need the negative explained in order for them to actually see what possibly could happen.

Promote The Preferred Future

Just as you must help people see the negative impact of not moving towards your presented offer, you also need to show them how an agreement can bring good things. Attach your proposal to the individual's goals and aspirations. Show how what you are bringing to the table will give him/her more success in life now and in the future.

Share The Consequences

Consequences don't have to be bad. A consequence is merely a result or a cause and effect that may be either positive or negative depending on the choice a person makes. This step often requires you to slow the process for comprehension. You need to be detailed, direct, and respectful.

Present A Call To Action

No persuasion event is complete until you have presented the call to action. People generally choose not to decide if they are not asked to. Present your case, check for clear understanding, detail the expectations, and provide a timeframe.

If you follow these steps, you will ensure successful persuasion. Remember: Always have Plan B ready to share as not everyone will buy-in the first time.

RELATIONSHIP

Relationship is the one vital foundational principle for influence, trust, and persuasion. If you do not establish and continue to build it, you will NEVER reach the level of influence you need to leave a positive legacy.

If you are struggling with gaining influence, look at your relationships with those you are trying to influence. Whenever two people come together in any setting, a relationship begins. Those in leadership endeavoring to gain a positive level of influence realize they first have to work on building a relationship. How do you successfully accomplish building a relationship in which positive influence is allowed by the other party?

When you begin to develop a relationship, there are things people look for in you, and there are things you need to offer. What is it people are looking for in you that indicates to them you are worthy of developing a relationship?

Tonality

Your tone of voice is important, especially with beginning interactions. If you do well in the beginning and then change, you lose your consistency and become unreliable. This destroys your relationship.

Validation

When building relationships and trying to keep them progressing, it is important that you find opportunities to validate the other person. In our society very seldom does someone get approved just for who he/she is. Everyone is of great value, and you must make him/her aware of that regularly.

Certainty

Do you display an air of certainty with your decisions and communication? People want to be able to trust the person with whom they are trying to establish a relationship. Being decisive and also considerate is something people value.

I remember one of our new leaders coming into a position within our organization as a District Leader. This was a new venture for him, so he only had surface level of knowledge of our industry. When he was hired, I knew he would have to make good relationships with the people whom he would interact with daily because he needed them for gaining understanding in order to lead that district into growth.

Things were going well until he met one employee who knew he had no knowledge of the business. She wasn't going to acknowledge his leadership or follow his attempts for improving her performance. What was he to do? He began by practicing tonality, validation, and certainty.

Once he knew he would have a problem building a relationship with this individual, he began watching and giving her genuine praise in a sincere tone that showed he noticed what she accomplished and appreciated it. The validation process opened up a good relationship and a trusted level of leadership. However, he had to make himself vulnerable to establish her validation. This isn't the case with everyone. She was a strong performer and knew much more than he did, so he took advantage of her strength.

It was the beginning of his fourth week on the job. When he walked in that Monday morning, he told the Store Manager he was on a learning-and-relationship building mission. As soon as the employee was ready for the day, he began a casual conversation asking her how she was and about her weekend. He shared with her that he had been observing her process and comparing it to other locations he had visited. If he wanted to learn the process correctly, she would be the one he wanted to use as a model.

She smiled, handed over the controls of the computer, and he began taking care of customers. Even the things he was confident with, he asked her to check his work. When others would ask why he was doing this and not having someone in the training department teach him, he told them his style of leadership was very relationship-oriented and hands-on. The best people to teach him were those on the frontline every day.

As he went from store to store in his district, he continued to use the steps of genuine tonality, validation, and certainty. Those actions combined with people's intrinsic needs made a cultural foundation that built a highly successful sales district within a matter of months.

Since we have discussed what people are looking for in others when they form relationships, let's now explore what their intrinsic needs are. We should be meeting these to make sure we are investing our best efforts in developing the relationship:

Honor Existence

Honoring existence is the most fundamental of human needs. In today's world most people feel as though they are treated as either just another number or totally insignificant. Those who honor others by noting their contributions and activities are those who influence other's lives. You must take time to notice things they do and listen to their stories. Know what is important to them and their goals. Show them they are not just a number to you.

Respect Fears

People have many fears such as social rejection, criticism of work, loss of stability, etc. If you are going to be allowed into the inner circle of a person, you have to respect his/her fears and help him/her find ways to defeat them. Regardless of how minor these fears may seem, they are huge to the person. He/she will welcome someone who respects what it means to him/her and helps to find solutions.

Champion Wants

The person who takes time to understand the wants of the individual who he/she is trying to build a relationship with and help him/her attain his/her goals will develop a long-lasting friendship. In a society that pushes people to look after their own goals, finding a person who is genuinely willing to invest time and energy into other people is rare.

THE DIMENSION MODEL

People who desire influential relationships are those who are willing to put the needs of others before themselves. It is establishing a bond that allows the other person to invest positive energy into their lives. You trust the other person to have only the best intentions in mind. This takes time. Attempting to build an influential relationship requires thinking about the relationship in three distinct dimensions.

Cognitive Dimension

How does the individual perceive my motives? What has he/she heard about me? What does my reputation say about me?

Emotional Dimension

Are there feelings the person has about me that I need to overcome? How does he/she feel about our relationship at work?

Behavioral Dimension

Do my actions support my words? What type of reaction am I seeing in our conversations?

When you invest the time to be aware of these various dimensions as well as what people are looking for and need in a relationship, you can truly make a difference in their lives because they will allow you the opportunity to do so. The key is to not push and never assume that you are owed the privilege of influence in anyone's life except your own. You must earn this privilege by placing them first.

FOUNDATIONAL PROCESS

Influence is defined as having the capacity to be a compelling force or produce effects on the actions, behavior, and opinions of others. In order to accomplish this, you must understand that all of the relationship considerations discussed in the previous parts of this chapter unfold during a three-stage foundational process of gaining influence with people.

Educational Phase

First, there is an educational phase. Here you help others see how to look at a specific issue or proposal and help them uncover the opportunity that lies within what you are sharing. People come to every situation in life with preconceived ideologies that are often times based on a short supply of information. It is up to you to give the much-needed information and help them to see how it can be to their advantage.

Challenge Phase

The next phase is the challenge phase. You have already shared details that have educated them about what is needed and its importance. Now you need to put forth a challenge that can fall in any or all of the following areas:

Be Better

Cause others to think about how following the proposed plan of action could allow them to become a better worker, more productive, or a better version of themselves. Many people when challenged to become better will rise to the occasion. Invest in the change process and their results will astound you.

Be True

This area can be multi-faceted. It may mean being true to themselves and their beliefs. It may mean being true to their job and/or employer. Help them recognize which one is more important and provide guidance.

Be Significant

A great number of people want to make a difference with their lives, but they don't think they can ever accomplish this. As a person trying to influence them, it is your job to make sure you help them achieve this level of significance. You do this by knowing what they can do and providing support and opportunities.

Lead By Example Phase

If you miss this final phase, all of your work means nothing and actually goes against you. Remember: There can never be two sets of rules. You are in this together, and if you want to achieve a high level of influence, they must see you do what you say.

TRUST

Trust is the backbone of influence. If people do not trust you, you will never be a person of positive influence to them. The definition of trust is a firm belief in the reliability or truth or strength etc. of a person or thing; a confident expectation. Basically it is the act of placing yourself in a vulnerable position of relying on others to treat you in a fair, open, and honest way.

A Harvard Business Review, (Kumar, 1996) publication, says, "[Trust] creates a reservoir of goodwill that helps preserve the relationship when, as will inevitably happen, one party engages in an act that its partner considers destructive." (n.p)

Trust is a difficult thing since it takes a long time to build but only moments to destroy. It is also difficult because we live in a very non-trusting world, and people are very cautious with extending trust.

Ways you can establish or re-establish trust:

Be the Trust Message

Do your actions align with your words?

Trust First

If you expect to build or rebuild trust, you have to take the first step. Trust is like a bridge spanning a deep divide; it is built one step at a time.

Model Accountability

We all make mistakes or poor decisions that impact others. It is not the mistake that discredits your trust; it is what you do with the mistake that makes the difference.

Build Relationships

Lasting relationships are often taken for granted in the workplace. Relationships are the backbone of influence that prosper only in an environment of trust.

Put Others First

When trust is growing, you will find those who are building it are focused with helping others achieve their goals, dreams, and aspirations.

Realize Your Impact

Everything we believe, each sentence we speak, and all of our actions impact those around us on a daily basis. We need to be always positively encouraging them.

Demonstrate Value

Everyone wants to feel needed and appreciated. We all have an inherent need to connect and feel valued. Giving people credit for a job well done, truly listening, and letting them know they are greatly appreciated is huge.

Some of the framework's parts incorporate other aspects mentioned throughout this chapter. It is important that you are aware of how all parts work together for a level of influence for growing your legacy.

Greater Trust = Greater Influence

As we close this chapter, I want to share some final tips about how to ensure you are gaining the level of influence you need as a leader. Your ability to influence hinges on your understanding of the following:

- The circumstances surrounding the event or person you are working with.
- The level of clarity they have about what you are trying to accomplish.
- The properly casting of the vision of what success looks like.
- The identification and verbalizing of the common ground you share with them.

If you will approach every relationship with the concepts discussed in this chapter, you are guaranteed to increase your level of influence. The reality of having a positive focus is centered on our choice to make a purposeful effort to help better people.

CHAPTER TAKEAWAYS

Influence

Those who have very little positive influence over those they lead have four general traits preventing them from having a long-lasting positive influence:

- They neglect building relationships based on the other person's good.
- They disconnect from those around them unless they want something.
- They are concerned with self and self-gain and have little room for anyone else.
- Their decisions are perceived as inconsistent.

Persuasion

Persuasion is utilized more as a negotiation technique. It is a temporary framework allowing you to achieve a certain goal in a moment of time. If handled correctly, these six crucial parts will allow you to be successful in any bargaining or negotiating situation:

- Be respectful.
- Deliver a specific benefit.
- Define the impact.
- Promote the preferred future.
- Share the consequences.
- Present a call to action.

When you begin to develop a relationship, there are things people look for in you, and there are things you need to offer:

- Tonality
- Validation
- Certainty

We should be meeting these intrinsic needs in order to make sure we are investing our best efforts in developing the relationship:

- Honor existence.
- Respect fears.
- Champion wants.

As we look to influence others, we need to put forth challenges to help people grow in a positive manner:

- Be better.
- Be true.
- Be significant.

Ways you can establish or re-establish trust:

- Be the trust message.
- Trust first.
- Model accountability.
- Build relationships.
- Put others first.
- Realize your impact.
- Demonstrate value.

5

The Conflict Resolution System

"Peace is not absence of conflict; it is the ability to handle conflict by peaceful means."

-President Ronald Reagan

O ccasionally even the best of friends can get into a conflict. Generally, these situations work themselves out if both sides value each other. However, when the situation involves people working together on a day-to-day basis, it can make things very difficult to resolve.

I remember when I was operating a group of retail stores, it seemed as though conflict with my store managers was a daily issue. They were always having difficulty with their team members, and they would alternate between motivating them by enticing them with a promised reward or threatening their job. This indecisiveness causes conflict, and handling it incorrectly makes it worse.

One manager in particular had this type of approach and was having problems with a sales associate not consistently meeting her numbers. It became apparent that nothing he was trying was working, and both individuals were frustrated with each other. When I observed this and mentioned it to him, he said, "I just don't know what to do to get around this issue and make it work. Any ideas?" It was then that I shared some of the principles of this chapter with him.

CONFLICT

Conflict is inevitable in any situation where people spend extended periods of time together. In a small business where roles are often highly interdependent, your ability to manage conflict and keep everybody working together is essential for success. Awareness of possible reasons for conflict can help you limit it in your workplace. It seems that in today's business world, workplace conflict come more frequently and impacts more people than ever before. A recent *CPP Global Human Capital Report* (Hayes, 2008) shows that the levels of workplace conflict in the U.S. are relatively high with 36% of employees having to deal with it always or frequently versus 29%

average across the world. The top two causes are 62% personality and ego clashes and 20% poor management practices. How does your workplace rate? What are the causes you see?

The good news is there are some core basics which will help you as the leader manage the conflict better and arrive at a resolution quicker. The relationship is the reason some differences never rise to the level of a heightened conflict stage. When two people work together, they form some level of a relationship. At some point a stimulus arrives and puts stress in that relationship. Depending on the value each person places on the relationship determines whether this stimulus will reach the conflict stage requiring resolution by outside factors or if the relationship is valued enough to talk through the situation.

Emotions

If a leader is aware that the individual holding the least value of the relationship generally determines which way the situation goes, it helps him/her understand the root cause of any conflict in the workplace. A leader should create a relational atmosphere within his/her workplace and encourage open, honest communication while modeling the practice of talking through issues. When people disagree with a statement, it triggers an emotional response in their brains. Everyone has four basic emotions:

- Happy
- Anger
- Fear
- Sadness

When we look at these emotions, it is vital for a leader to understand that three out of the four will trigger an emotional response releasing the chemical cortisol into the brain. The release of cortisol is the human body's natural response to fight-or-flight. When cortisol is released, your heart rate goes up, muscles tense, and the brain goes into hyper-active mode. This causes us to become very sensitive to others around us, not to think logically, and to become stressed. Often times the parties involved are working with a perceived threat and not a real, physical, manifested threat.

Understanding Conflict

We define conflict as a disagreement through which those involved perceive a threat to their needs, interests, or concerns. For understanding this better, consider the following:

Disagreement

Generally, there is some level of difference in the positions of the two (or more) individuals involved in the conflict. The **TRUE** issue versus the **PERCEIVED** issue may be quite different from one another. In fact, conflict tends to be accompanied by varying levels of misunderstanding that exaggerate things considerably. Understanding the true areas of disagreement will help us solve the right problems and manage the real needs.

Parties Involved

It is important to understand that, in general, conflict is not just confined to the people verbally sharing their different feelings. Due to the structure of most organizations, numerous people are sharing the same workspace and thus are able to hear the conflict. Often if they do not hear it firsthand, they will be introduced to it secondhandedly. As a leader you have to listen and be aware that others are also experiencing the fallout from this conflict.

Perceived Threat

In most workplace conflicts people respond to the perceived threat. In the last few years workplace conflict has begun to include unfortunate displays of violence. While perception doesn't become reality all of the time, people's behaviors, feelings, and responses adjust to the evolving sense of the threat they perceive. When you attempt to work within the confines of conflict resolution, realizing the individual's perspective of the situation will greatly speed positive results.

Needs, Interests, or Concerns

There is a tendency to narrowly define "the problem" as one of substance, task, and near-term situations. However, workplace conflicts tend to be far more complex than that because they involve ongoing relationships with complex components.

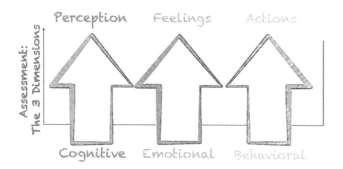

THE DIMENSION MODEL

Cognitive Dimension- Perception

These are our ideas and thoughts about a conflict often presented as inner voices.

Emotional Dimension- Feelings

These are the feelings, ranging from anger and fear to despair and confusion, we experience in conflict. Emotional responses are often misunderstood as people tend to believe others feel the same as they do.

Behavioral Dimension- Actions

These responses can play an important role in our ability to meet our needs in the conflict. Caused by cortisol release when we sense a threat, they may include heightened stress, bodily tension, increased perspiration, tunnel vision, shallow or accelerated breathing, nausea, and rapid heartbeat. This causes us to act out in a manner to defend our position and occasionally causes us to say and do things we later regret as our cortisol levels return to normal.

PERCEPTION

Any efforts to resolve conflicts effectively must take these points into account. However, the hardest one to factor in and define the particulars of is perception because each party may have a different perspective of any given situation. Here are a few factors that may skew one's perception and must be considered when trying to determine root causes in any conflict:

Culture, Race, and Ethnicity

Our different cultural backgrounds cause us to hold differing beliefs about society as well as the role of conflict in that experience. How individuals react in the face of conflict and the subsequent resolution phase can be very different. The leader has to look at what influence this may have with the attempts to understand, recognize, and resolve the issues.

Gender

Based on men's and women's experiences in the world, they perceive situations differently. Men and women will often approach conflict situations with differing mindsets about the desired outcomes as well as the set of possible solutions.

Knowledge Base

People respond to conflicts based on their real time and experiential knowledge they may have about the issue. This influences their openness to engage in managing the conflict. Either they will be open to a win-win proposition, or they will undermine any efforts to bring about resolution.

Previous Experiences

Many have had significant life experiences that continue to influence their perceptions of current reality. These experiences may have left them fearful, non-trusting, and reluctant to agree with possible joint solutions. Previous experiences can be a powerful resource of positive reactions leaving them confident, open to taking chances, and moving into a win-win partnership agreement in order to solve the situation. Either way the role of previous experiences must be taken into consideration as a forming element of our perception.

Generational Differences

Every generation perceives and reacts differently to the same stimuli of a conflict. Since we can easily find four distinct generations working in the exact same place and time, this is a top consideration when thinking about how involved parties are identifying what is actually happening. Any leader in today's workplace must have a good understanding of generational perception in order to work through conflicts.

These factors work to form the perceptions through which employees experience conflict. As a result, the reactions to the threat and stress posed by conflict should be expected to include varying views of the same situation. This also means there will be significant misunderstanding of each other's perceptions, needs, and feelings. These challenges contribute to our overall feelings during conflict. Thus the situation is overwhelming and unsolvable, so resolution is often seen as too hard and ultimately is avoided.

Now that we understand the contributing factors that develop our perceptions of conflict and what leads to most conflicts, what do we do?

In order to solve any conflict, you have to go back and examine which of the dimensions, Cognitive, Emotional or Behavioral, is most heavily working to agitate the current situation. To focus on what is most predominate and knowing how to proceed, ask yourself these questions:

Cognitive Dimension

- How do the parties perceive or think about this conflict?
- What data are they focusing on? What are their conclusions about this data?
- What assumptions have they made? Why?

- What is the tone and theme of the way they explain the conflict?
- What motives have they attributed to the other party? What data might contradict this perception?
- How are these perceptions affecting the thoughts, feelings, and behaviors of the other parties?
- What would change each party's view of the problem?

Emotional Dimension:

- What are the parties feeling about this conflict?
- What is the depth of these feelings? How much venting is taking place or is needed?
- How significant are these feelings to resolution?
- What are the emotional triggers necessary between the parties?
- What does each person need in order to let go of these feelings?
- How are these feelings affecting the perceptions and behaviors of the other parties?
- What would change how everyone felt?

Behavioral Dimension

- What actions has each party taken to deal with the conflict?
- What behaviors are escalating the conflict? What behaviors are de-escalating the conflict?
- What behavioral triggers are in place?
- What is the risk of aggression or violence?
- What is the risk of withdrawal and avoidance?
- How are these feeling affecting the actions, feelings, and perceptions of the other parties?
- What would change everyone's behavior?

As you progress your way through the three dimensions, you will soon begin to see either one that rises above the rest or a few elements from each one that need to be addressed. Determine what is the most important aspect that must be addressed first and focus your energy in that area. The important part to remember is the perceptions of each involved party will play a large role in addressing where this situation goes from here. Since you have already examined that aspect, use what you have learned to formulate an action plan that is mutually beneficial.

FORWARD THINKING

Action plans are crucial to formulating a winning resolution. The best way to accomplish this is through a process called Forward Thinking.

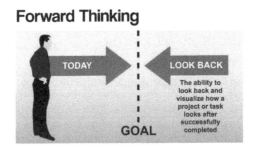

This involves envisioning the optimal outcome of the action plan and then mentally moving forward to that place. Consider these factors:

- What does the preferred outcome look like?
- How will the parties involved feel about it?
- How should I expect them to react?
- How much follow-up will I need to do once the resolution is put into place?

Once you have envisioned the best possible outcome, ask yourself what the final stage of the conversations would be just before reaching the actual resolution:

- Do the parties seem to buy into the proposed resolution?
- How much have I allowed them to be a part of designing the resolution?
- Is this going to be a true win-win for all parties? If not, how can we get there?
- Does it seem that the parties are actually resolving this situation, or are they just trying to get finished with the process?

This process will continue as you mentally work your way backwards to the point you were when you first began to address the conflict. This is the reverse of how we typically do things. We normally have a goal we want to reach, and we try to figure out how we are going to do this. In forward thinking we reach the goal and consider all the steps involved in a successful journey. By working backwards things become much clearer and also allow us to anticipate obstacles.

As you continue to build an action plan, remember these important things:

Buy-In

This is one of the most important factors in determining the overall success of the resolution you develop. Leaders often want to design what the plan will be and then tell those involved what their role in it will be. However, if the leader will take the time to ask those involved what they could do to make a difference and then incorporate that into the plan, success is nearly automatic.

Dimensions

Just as conflict has three major dimensions, your action plan needs to resolve any issues within these three dimensions. If you address a few issues and do not resolve all the areas that are triggers, you will have more conflict later with the same issues.

Equality

It takes two or more to have a conflict, and all need to have an equal share in the resolution. Very seldom will a good action plan have one person changing his/her actions, thoughts, or feelings more than the others involved. If you find the plan is suddenly becoming too slanted in favor of one party, change it and explain why all must give equally.

Follow-up

Setting a follow-up date to meet with the parties involved is crucial. If there is no time arranged for the individuals to meet with the leader and communicate the progress or lack of progress, nothing will ever happen to bring about full resolution. The leader must assess the ongoing process on a daily basis to ensure things are moving along as planned. Brief five-minute conversations with those involved will easily indicate if progress is being made in a timely manner. If you have set a formal follow-up date at thirty days, there has to be an informal follow-up around the twenty-day mark. Why? A leader should always understand that his/her job is to help the employee be successful. What good would it do to anyone involved in the conflict resolution if the leader waited until the thirtieth day and told the employee he/she failed or brought a failing report to the meeting? However, if the leader meets informally at the twentieth-day mark and sees issues left unresolved, then he/she can remind those involved that the resolution is to be completed by the thirtieth day. This also allows everyone to pull together in order to make a speedy resolve of anything left undone.

COSTS OF CONFLICT

Conflict is a real and unfortunate result of people working together and personalities clashing. It has been estimated that workplace conflict costs U.S. employers one billion dollars a year through high employee turnover, absentee or frequently sick employees, increased employee litigation, low morale, and decreased productivity.

Hard Costs

These are measurable costs that can be deducted from your financial statements. Though they're tangible and usually easy to find and calculate, managers often overlook them in the midst of conflict.

Wasted Time

Time is money. If people are avoiding one another and delaying outcomes, there's a cost to that.

Lost Workdays

If you're expecting people who are in conflict (or who are surrounded by conflict) to work without resolution, they may be taking sick days just to avoid the stress.

Reduced Productivity

When you have to work on a project with someone you're not getting along with, the job takes longer and the final product is affected.

Performance And Quality

Even if you don't notice a marked drop in productivity, you'll probably notice a diminished quality in the work.

Healthcare Costs

Some workplace stressors may not be avoidable, but allowing the stress of unresolved conflict to continue only adds to the pressures your employees may already face.

Sabotage And Theft

If employees reach a point where they feel no one cares about a situation, it's not all that unusual for sabotage and theft to happen.

Turnover

Regardless of the size of your organization, there's a dollar amount associated with the cost of hiring, processing, and training every new employee.

Termination Packages

Unresolved conflict can lead to a termination package which costs the company more than if someone stays or leaves on good terms.

Legal Costs

If a lawsuit is filed, you'll spend money on legal fees and wages for all the employees who are involved in the court case. The money you pay out isn't going toward productivity or more sales.

Soft Costs

These are things that may not seem measurable or easily assigned a specific dollar amount, but they still affect your profits.

Morale

People are likely aware of an ongoing conflict, and this awareness can affect morale.

Decreased Customer Service

Taking care of employees who interact with customers keeps clients satisfied.

Reputation

Word travels quickly when people find a great enterprise who really values its employees. Disgruntled employees' comments can discourage future valued employees and potential customers.

Loss Of Skilled Employees

Retaining skilled employees keeps production high and training time to a minimum.

Let's take the following example of the cost of losing a single mid-level employee due to conflict within a hypothetical organization with 100 employees and apply the Dana Cost Calculator from figures generated by HR Magazine, (Administrator, 2003):

Employee's annual salary: **$80,000**

Multiply by 1.4 (140%) as the investment you have in the employee: **$112,000**

Multiply by 1.5 (150%) as the cost of replacing the employee: **$168,000**

Multiply by .6 (60%) average role of conflict in voluntary terminations: **$100,800**

Multiply times the number of voluntary terminations in your organization annually

A 10% turnover rate in a company of 100 employees is 10 employees.

10 X $100,800 = ***$1,008,000***

What an amazing loss to the organization! If this was any other type of line item on a profit and loss statement, it would not be tolerated by leaders. Because management is usually not aware of this, it is considered a hidden loss.

At the beginning of this chapter, I told you about one of my managers who was having problems with a sales associate not consistently meeting her numbers. After I had a discussion with the manager, he realized that while he was trying to lead the sales associate to results, he had not developed a good, healthy working relationship with her. Utilizing the Forward Thinking approach, he was able to practice conversations and possible objections that might arise.

Soon she was regularly meeting her goals, and their relationship grew to an increased trust level. While she was never the top seller, she became someone the manager could count on.

It has been proven that organizations which take the time to train their leadership about how to effectively deal with workplace conflict are the organizations that see less of all the previous mentioned things. They also experience greater profitability and sustainability as their employees can function in a positive, growing environment. We still see organizations leaning towards ignoring conflict instead of dealing with it. It may seem easier to avoid it in the present, but it is definitely defining the future of your organization. The future will not look as bright for those who would rather avoid conflict issues versus those who choose to create a solid action plan.

CHAPTER TAKEAWAYS

Relationships

The value each person places on the relationship will determine whether this stimulus will reach the conflict stage which requires resolution by outside factors or if each person values the relationship enough to talk through the situation.

Dimensions

There are three basic areas you must consider regardless of what the conflict is centered around:

- Cognitive Dimension- Perception
- Emotional Dimension- Feelings
- Behavioral Dimension- Actions

Perception

Here are a few factors that skew one's perception and must be considered when trying to determine root causes in any conflict:

- Culture, race, and ethnicity
- Gender
- Knowledge Base
- Differences
- Previous experiences
- Generational

Forward Thinking

Action plans are crucial to formulating a winning resolution. The best way to accomplish this is through a process called Forward Thinking. As you continue to build an action plan, remember these few important things:

- Buy-in
- Dimensions

- Equality
- Follow-up

Hard Costs

These are measurable costs that can be deducted from your financial statements. Though they're tangible and usually easy to find and calculate, managers often overlook them in the midst of conflict.

- Wasted time
- Lost workdays
- Reduced productivity
- Performance and quality
- Healthcare costs associated with stress

- Sabotage and theft
- Turnover
- Termination packages
- Legal costs

Soft Costs

These are things that may not seem measurable or easily assigned a specific dollar amount, but they still affect your profits:

- Morale
- Decreased customer service
- Reputation
- Loss of skilled employees

6

The Strategic Organizational Playbook

"Planning is bringing the future into the present so that you can do something about it now."

-Alan Lakein

There's a saying, "He who fails to plan is planning to fail." It is attributed to many people and is very true.

In the constantly changing and demanding world of business, leaders have to become very good at strategic planning and then communicating that plan. More often we see business owners or leaders attempting to tackle a new year without taking the steps to formally craft a Strategic Business Plan complete with goals and Key Performance Indicators (KPIs) in order to lead their business into new growth opportunities. Before I began to follow a strategic planning process, my business was progressing, but I knew there was more to achieve. However, I couldn't figure out how to do this. What I had been missing for so long was connecting core values, vision statement, mission statement, strategic goals, and my team into one linked, purposeful machine.

I remember one morning I was meeting with all of my leaders. We were determined to come away from our two-day strategy meeting with a plan that would lead us to success in the coming year. It was important that we come up with solid strategies as the organization had been struggling the last two years, and it was time for change.

As we met to review our core values and existing vision statement, I could tell we were at a critical point. The energy in the room was very tense, and it seemed that at any moment arguments would ensue. As the leader of this group of dedicated professionals, it was my responsibility to bring direction and purpose but most of all hope.

We had finished affirming our current values and vision. Now it was time to change the mission statement to reflect the upcoming challenges. Each year we would choose a new mission statement combined with different goals for the company, and in a later meeting we would begin to divide the goals into KPIs for each of our store locations. We involved the staff at the store level by having them make fun, engaging scoreboards for tracking purposes.

Those couple of days were filled with ideas, emotions, passion, and success. We were able to connect to a shared mission which drove the team because they felt involved and knew they could make a difference. One of the crucial aspects of making your plan work within your organization is achieving buy-in with your leaders. The more involved they are in formulating parts of the plan, the more successful they will be with getting their team on board.

We left those meetings with a team desiring to do well for themselves and the company. I sent them out with an impassioned plea for excellence from each of the locations and a speech about how this year would be one of our best.

In this chapter I will share with you the steps we followed and also some checks and balances which led to one of our most profitable years.

CORE VALUES

The first thing we did was to ensure that our established organizational values were still relevant as the company had grown. Core values, the guiding principles that dictate behavior and action, can help companies determine if they are on the right path and fulfilling their business goals because core values create an unwavering and unchanging guide.

Any organization can move forward without core values, but you will move forward much faster and solve more problems if you have these foundational values. Having an established set of core values guides all decisions you face.

Why core values matter:

- Improve morale and are a rich source of individual and organizational pride
- Align a large group of people around specific, idealized behaviors
- Guide difficult decisions by determining priorities in advance
- Attract, hire, and retain the right type of employees
- Prevent and mitigate conflicts that do arise
- Differentiate your brand in the minds of your customers and partners

The following is our company's, Mid-America Wireless, core values which were carried over from the previous year:

- Excellent Customer Service
- Integrity
- Open Communication
- Teamwork

VISION

Our vision statement was also carried over from the previous year:

Mid-America Wireless is the communication connection between you, your world, and beyond.

Our vision statement indicated that we believed regardless of the type of communication you were having, we would be that connection not only within your circle of family and friends but also to the rest of the world. We would be your preferred communication provider.

The word *vision* is defined as "the act of anticipating that which will be or may come to be."

The vision statement states what ultimately the leadership envisions the business to be in terms of growth, values, employees, and contributions to society. Your vision statement is a broad look at the intended impact your organization will make. Your mission statement is how you utilize the vision statement daily to ensure it holds true.

When crafting a vision statement or revisiting it, ask the following questions:

- What is the positive impact my organization will have on our customers?
- What sets us apart from the competition? (Some will say they have no competition, but in reality whether you are non-profit, school, church, etc., people can always go somewhere else.)
- Envisioning your organization as a success and impacting everyone in a positive manner, how will your employees benefit from working for you?
- What are some buzzwords used by people who do business with you if your values are working well?

Next, examine your answers along with your values and begin to craft a one-to-three sentence vision for your organization. A vision statement is much like the sunset. You can drive forever towards the sunset but never reach it. However, as you are driving towards it, you are making progress.

If you have done well, you should be able to share your vision statement in sixty seconds or less. The goal is to intrigue people enough to say, "Tell me how you do that." You want to give people just enough information to pique their interest in your concept. This allows you to then move into what your organization is all about and how you can help solve their issues and problems.

This will give you a great look at how you are going to be able to review or create your organization's vision statement. It is a great start, but if you leave it here, you will never make progress. The vision has to reach reality through some means which is the mission statement. A vision statement for a business sets your goals at a high level.

MISSION

We crafted our mission statement during our planning meeting:

Creating "Moments of Magic" for our internal and external guests while achieving a top five ranking among AT&T agents within our region.

The mission statement is a concise statement of your business strategy and developed so that it puts things into action which will directly make your vision operational. The mission statement should answer three questions:

- What do we do?
- How do we do it?
- For whom do we do it?

In order to help craft an impactful mission statement, consider the following questions and answer them very specifically:

- What problem(s) do you solve? What need(s) do you fulfill?
- How are you unique from everyone else? What is your unique selling proposition? What makes you stand out?
- What factors from your vision statement should you keep in mind when writing your mission statement?
- What are the measures of success/key performance indicators? How will you know you have succeeded?

Next combine your winning idea and success measures into a general but measurable statement. Refine the words until you have a concise statement that expresses your ideas, measures, and desired result.

This process truly helps you visualize a positive, preferred track for your organization in the year to come. One factor of the human brain is the continued thought string. This means that as you move through a project, you have to continue to bring the most important parts of the previous step to the current step in order to maintain continuity and avoid becoming sidetracked. During strategic planning it is easy to lose focus and begin to drift in purpose and plan. The next two steps will help you to not only stay on track but also to think even deeper about your future destination.

PURPOSE

Not long ago a business leader friend of mine was struggling with moving to the next plateau of his business. He was already very successful and had been for a few years. However, there was a very evident ceiling his organization struggled to break through and frustration had set in. In our conversation I asked him a simple question that I ask all organizations and individuals I coach or work with. It ended up being the catalyst that allowed him to break through the ceiling.

When I am coaching individuals, the "magic" question I ask is "Why do you exist?" When working with organizations, I ask, "What is the primary reason your organization exists?" If your answer is based around money or a product, you will ALWAYS hit a ceiling. Your flow of money will ebb and flow depending upon the many issues you may have, and someone will always be willing to discount more than you and acquire supplies at a lower price. Therefore, money cannot be the primary reason because it is a constantly moving target that occasionally you have no control over.

Let's say you are feeling that a particular product or product line is why your organization exists. What happens when the demand falls for the product? Consider what happens when your competition does something even greater than you have. Product-based existence is limited in both longevity and function. In order to have a lasting purpose, it has to be based around what you or your organization can do for your clients. Consider these questions:

- What is your niche?
- What do we do better than anyone else?

You have to be differentiating yourself every day. Each day you want those who interact with you to walk away inspired to tell everyone with similar needs that your organization is the ONLY place to go. This is true for both your external and internal clients.

After this conversation my friend realized he had been looking at his construction business in the wrong way. He thought his purpose was to build a great house made out of the best products in a very timely manner. While that was exactly what he did, he missed the deeper reason that made his company so successful.

We all fall into the trap of missing the WHY in what we do. I asked him to tell me why he thought his clients wanted the best products they could get. What was the point in making sure that he delivered a top quality home to his clients? Naturally, he said that his clients wanted great value for their money. True, but there is more. I asked him to think about why it was important to have a good quality home. What benefits and assurances were in it for his clients? He began to list all of the protections the family had through storms. He mentioned he built in security measures for the safety of the family. That was the moment he realized his business was not as much about building homes as it was delivering peace of mind, safety, and security for those who hired him. He changed his marketing from being product-based to benefit-based and his sales increased dramatically.

Once this mental block was removed, we went through many other questions. Before he could thoroughly answer these questions, he needed to understand the process of Forward Thinking.

Forward Thinking

This mental process allows you to move forward to a point where you have successfully achieved or exceeded your goal, envisioning what success looks and feels like, and what the organization is experiencing. Once you have a firm grip with that vision, you can then start working backwards step-by-step to where you are setting the goal. Taking the time to go forward and working your way backwards have been key success factors for many people in both personal and professional life.

"The Compass Analyzer" ™

"The Compass Analyzer" ™ helps find true direction. The next phase looks deeply into the revenue and profit stream. While the purpose should not be exclusively dedicated to money, the revenue stream can be a good tracking mechanism for the purpose of realizing the product and service offerings.

These questions helped turn my friend's construction company into a breakthrough organization:

- What specifically will the company look like in three years? In five years?
- What are the current issues facing the company?
- What are the three most important goals for the company over the next 90 days? Who is responsible for their accomplishment?
- Who is the target market? What proven processes make you successful? Why?

"Your Strategic Vision" ™

In order to make sure you stay headed in the correct direction, we designed a product called "Your Strategic Vision" ™. The reasoning is to take quality vision and mission statements and develop those into workable, realistic goals and key performance indicators (KPIs).

During my company's two-day strategy meeting, it was important for us to firmly understand who our customers were. This is discovering the WHO behind the target market. In our case it was the teenager, soccer-mom, business owner, executive on the move, families that are spread over distances, etc. As a wireless phone organization, we had to think of everyone who used our product and why.

Next, we began looking at all of our programs, products, and services that were currently profitable and why. Which specific phones were selling? Which were most profitable? What about the accessories, service plans, satellites, etc.? Based on our vision, mission, and customers we had to ask, "What services or products should we be providing to create more value for our customers?" Since we did not create the devices or accessories for the services, we had to look at things which we could directly influence. It is important when you make your goals and KPIs that you craft them in a way allowing your organization full impact and responsibility for success. You will end buy-in if your goals or KPIs are subject to third party input for success.

At this point my leaders were in a position to list the top five products and services which would push our organization forward in the coming year. We had defined our customers, identified our purpose, revealed what was currently successful, and what was needed to move us forward. We began to list our top five products asking ourselves what could we do that would make us more successful.

KPIs (Key Performance Indicators)

This brought us to the point where we needed to craft our goals and create the KPIs that would help us reach these.

Avoid these mistakes when crafting your KPIs:

Too vague

The goal doesn't identify specific waymarks that indicate not only when it is reached but also the reasoning.

Based On Wants, Not Facts

For example, saying you will grow sales 50% over last year, but you have only grown 15% in your best year. This is a want, not a fact.

Short-Term Thinking Only

It might seem this is a great idea, but can your organization withstand the move in the mid to long-term? For example, a restaurant that needs to increase profits waters down its product and keeps the price the same. Yes, the near-term profits go up, but in the long-term, business goes down as customers recognize the compromise.

Lack Of Priorities

It is difficult for humans to concentrate and perform at excellent levels on more than three things at once. Determine what things are the most important and move forward in these areas. When you reach success, add a new item one at a time.

Lack Of Communication

Goals should be posted, communicated, and tracked on an ongoing basis. When you first produce your goals, share them with all who are impacted or have physical input. Share why the goals are important and how each department or person makes a direct impact.

No Tracking Or Follow-Up

You need to talk about your goals at every staff meeting. If you don't keep it in the forefront of your team's mind, they will soon forget about the goal's significance.

Goals And KPIs

The 4 Disciplines of Execution, (Covey and Colosimo, 2005) uses "Wildly Important Goals," a Franklin-Covey term showing that goals are to be devised from your mission just as the mission is formulated from your vision. Remember: Your goals should start as yearly goals so they can be broken into 90-day increments. This allows your team to see a manageable goal. It also shows quicker progress than trying to reach a large number by the end of the year. You should have no more than three goals for the year. Every goal at every level must contain a clearly measurable result as well as the date for achievement. For example, a revenue-focused goal might be

"Increase percent of annual revenue from new products from 15 percent to 21 percent by December 31."

The formula to follow is **X to Y by (when).**

In our two-day meeting we came up with two Wildly Important Goals (WIG) that would propel us back to the award-winning organization we once were

- Each store will achieve a 5% increase of the gross margin average measured quarterly through December 31.

- Our team will enhance the culture of our organization by improving our company's cultural assessment score from 3.57 to 4 measured on a quarterly basis by December 31.

How were we going to accomplish these? A process of designing clear KPIs and focused lead indicators are critical to ensure consistent success. These KPIs should be crafted in a way that each department or business unit can own them and see their individual impact making a difference as the organization moves towards accomplishing the goals. If you are not a large organization with many departments, create them for the entire organization to work towards.

When crafting your KPIs, it is important not to be vague. Well-crafted KPIs should be

- Specific and clear
- Explicitly linked to purpose
- Plan language
- Bite-sized chunks
- Measurable
- Deadline-driven

Here you see our Wildly Important Goals (WIG) along with their accompanying KPIs and lead indicators. Lead indicators are predictable actions that if done consistently will lead to the success of the KPI. This will lead to a successful goal attainment helping you achieve mission and vision statements.

WIG 1

Each store will achieve a 5% increase of the gross margin average measured quarterly through December 31.

Lead 1

Each team member will complete a minimum of five prospecting presentations daily.

Lead 2

Every store team leader will participate in weekly sales training focuses with every team member.

WIG 2

Our team will enhance the culture of our organization by improving our company's cultural assessment score from 3.57 to 4 measured on a quarterly basis by December 31.

Lead 1

All leaders will deliver performance reviews to every team member on a quarterly basis by the 15th of the following month.

Lead 2

Through a pre-determined action plan, each store team leader will visit five different locations to develop a consistent, synergistic work environment by December 31.

Lead 3

All team members will participate in a team building exercise quarterly during the companywide training events through December 31.

If you have multiple departments, each department may have its own goals and KPIs to enhance the organizational overall goal as well. As a result of this process, we had one of the most profitable years and won many awards for our performance. The WIN was the fact that we lowered our turnover rate by 60% because we had buy-in from the leaders and teams. The culture was improved rapidly as each employee knew he/she made a difference and had direct impact on our vision and mission statements. We examined our company-wide hiring process, compared it to our new core values, vision and mission, and quickly realized we needed to revise them.

Scoreboards

How did we achieve the important task of getting our local teams excited and behind the WIGs and KPIs we had established in the meeting? We asked each team to design its own personalized store scoreboard for tracking the progress of the KPIs. If the teams were successful in meeting the KPIs, the goals would fall into place. The process for making a scoreboard is simple. You can have a computer-based software scoreboard, or you can make very basic ones to hang in the breakroom. Here is the process for successful scoreboard creation:

- Identify #1 KPI and predictable activities.
- Choose scoreboard type.
- Construct scoreboard.
- Make sure scoreboard is visible.
- Share, post, and measure it.

It is important that you place measurable activities, which your team is solely responsible for and doesn't have to rely on any outward party to attain success, on your scoreboard.

There are numerous types of scoreboards that you can design. They can be as simple as happy or sad faces, a thermometer, or a race track. The best performing scoreboards have often been laminated poster board. The key is to keep them simple. If the scoreboard is hard to use, track, or understand, it will mean nothing to the team, and they will not use them.

Always place the scoreboard in a very visible, accessible place so it is seen daily by all employees. Utilize bright colors and try not to have a large amount of things posted around it.

Your scoreboard needs to be talked about, shared throughout the company, and updated daily or however often the KPI indicates. The leader is responsible for maintaining the focus of this part of the overall plan. If it slides even once, the team will begin to lose interest. Remember: It takes at least twenty-one days to form a new habit. Make sure a different team member updates the scoreboard each time. The more people taking part in the process, the easier to maintain buy-in.

The golden rule for scoreboards is

"If you can't look at it and know you are winning or losing in under five seconds, redo it."

Excitement and fun are the key to success with scoreboards. When you make a significant move forward, celebrate if logistically realistic. If nothing else, make sure leadership shows genuine appreciation for the progress. When you have team meetings, make the scoreboard a part of it and always be encouraging about reaching the WIGs and KPIs. Always celebrate even the smallest of wins.

PLANNING

The November 30, 2011, <u>Forbes</u> article (Aileron, 2011) reported the following top five reasons most organizations find their planning session failed and did not yield the desired results:

- Having a plan simply for plan's sake
- Partial commitment
- No accountability or follow through
- Unrealistic goals or lack of focus and resources
- Unwillingness or inability to change

The strategic planning process and its corresponding results rest solely upon the leadership and owners of the organization. The highest level of leadership needs to be talking about the plan, sharing results, and following up on the scoreboards all year long. As critical as strategic planning is to the success of your company, all plans are useless unless followed by action. An additional side benefit of strategic planning is the natural action plan that stems from identifying the preferred strategy. While strategic planning involves your vision, mission and goals, it also further defines the rudiments of your action plan in order to achieve your desired results.

Some astonishing statistics from Mission Facilitators International (Statistics About Strategic Planning, n.d.) that stress the importance of taking time to work through strategic planning with your organization regardless of the size:

- Businesses using strategic plans are 12% more profitable. (1)
- Of 26,000 start-up business failures, 67% had no written plan. (2)
- In companies surveyed who used formal strategic planning processes, 64% of leaders said the planning led to strategic decisions allowing the company to meet its goals and challenges. (3)
- The top 10% of large companies surveyed experienced real and material benefits from their planning processes far

- beyond those of average companies. They have enjoyed improved control over costs, increased foresight, improved operational performance, increased transparency and insight into the business, and a sense of shared purpose. (4)
- Currently, 95% of the typical workforce doesn't understand the organization's strategy. (5)

Is it a great deal of work. However, the rewards you receive for faithfully working on the plan cannot be received through any other method.

CHAPTER TAKEAWAYS

Why Core Values Matter:

- Improve morale and are a rich source of individual and organizational pride
- Align a large group of people around specific, idealized behaviors
- Guide difficult decisions by determining priorities in advance
- Attract, hire, and retain the right type of employees
- Prevent and mitigate conflicts that arise
- Differentiate your brand in the minds of your customers and partners

When crafting a vision statement or revisiting it, ask the following questions:

- What is the positive impact my organization will have on our customers?
- What sets us apart from the competition? (Some will say they have no competition, but in reality whether you are non-profit, school, church, etc., people can always go somewhere else.)
- Envisioning your organization as a success and impacting everyone in a positive manner, how will your employees benefit from working for you?
- What are some buzzwords used by people who do business with you if your values are working well?

In order to help craft an impactful mission statement, consider the following questions and answer them very specifically:

- What problem(s) do you solve? What need(s) do you fulfill?
- How are you unique from everyone else? What is your unique selling proposition? What makes you stand out?

- What factors from your vision statement should you keep in mind when writing your mission statement?
- What are the measures of success/key performance indicators? How will you know you have succeeded?

Avoid these mistakes when making goals:

- Too vague
- Based on wants, not facts
- Short-term thinking only
- Lack of priorities
- Lack of communication
- No tracking or follow-up

CONCLUSION

I thank you for joining me on this journey. Since the end of 2012, I have been blest with the opportunity to follow my passion of sharing my knowledge. I have learned a lot about myself and continue to learn new things each day to help me in my career of coaching, training, and speaking.

My number one reason for writing this book was to share knowledge with you. I do not have all the answers, but when we are willing to learn, grow and change, our lives will improve. The framework of The High Achiever Mindset is based on Energy + Connections + Influence + Integrations = Great Results/Purpose of Life.

I normally ask my audiences, "Who in this room is a leader?" Only about 50% of the room will raise their hand. I am a firm believer we each should raise our hand because we are all leaders of ourselves. We all must decide the leadership we will show and share.

The High Achiever Leadership Formula has the six ingredients to help you become an inspiring and influential leader in your personal and professional life. As you finish this book, share it with others who would benefit from its contents. I had a mentor who gave me a book he thought would be beneficial. Ever since, I have been sharing books with others because I feel it is one way I can make a difference in someone's life.

As I close this book, I want you to follow my mantra: CHARGE (Create Habits Around Real Goals Everyday). You have the ability to become the person you want to be if you are willing to create a climber mindset in your daily life.

"It's your life. Why not live the life you want to live?"

-Gary Wilbers

Make it a GREAT day!

BIBLIOGRAPHY

10 shocking stats about disengaged employees (2014) Available at: https://www.officevibe.com/blog/disengaged-employees-infographic (Accessed: 29 August 2016).

Administrator (2003) *Best website on HRM - excellent HR tools and HR presentation slides - HR ppt - human resource management.* Available at: http://www.explorehr.org/articles/HR_Powerpoint_Slides/Management_Skills_and_HR_Management_Series.html (Accessed: 29 August 2016).

Aileron (2011) '10 reasons why strategic plans fail', *Forbes* (November),.

Antariksa, Y. (no date) 'Strategical Analysis: Overcoming Resistance To Change', *Exploring HR Management*, Available at: http://www.explorehr.org/articles/Organization_Analysis/Overcoming_Resistance_to_Change.html (Accessed: 29 August 2016).

Baumeister, R.F. and Tierney, J. (2011) *Willpower: Rediscovering the greatest human strength.* New York: Penguin Putnam.

Bigelow, J. and Poremba, A. (2014) 'Achilles' ear? Inferior human short-term and recognition memory in the Auditory modality', *PLoS ONE*, 9(2), p. e89914. doi: 10.1371/journal.pone.0089914.

Boundless (2016) *AIDA model.* Available at: https://www.boundless.com/marketing/textbooks/boundless-marketing-textbook/integrated-marketing-communications-12/introduction-to-integrated-marketing-communications-81/aida-model-406-4060/ (Accessed: 29 August 2016).

Covey, S.R. (1989) *The 7 habits of highly effective people: Powerful lessons in personal change.* New York: Simon and Schuster.

Covey, S.R. and Colosimo, J. (2005) *The 4 disciplines of execution a new workshop providing answers for today's greatest challenges.* United States: Franklin Covey Co.

Daily Mentoring for Achievers (no date) Available at: http://darrendaily.com (Accessed: 29 August 2016).

BIBLIOGRAPHY
(Continued)

Davenport, T.H. and Beck, J.C. (2001) *The attention economy: Understanding the new currency of business.* 2nd edn. Boston, MA: Harvard Business School Press.

Duhigg, C. (2012) *The power of habit: Why we do what we do in life and business.* New York: Random House Publishing Group.

Goleman, D. and Goleman, P.D. (2013) *Focus: The hidden driver of excellence.* New York, NY: HarperCollins Publishers.

Harry Chapin (1975) *Cat's in the cradle [Live 1975 Version]* .

Hayes, J. (no date) *WORKPLACE CONFLICT AND HOW BUSINESSES CAN HARNESS IT TO THRIVE.* Available at: https://www.cpp.com/pdfs/CPP_Global_Human_Capital_Report_Workplace_Conflict.pdf (Accessed: 29 August 2016).

Kumar, N. (1996) 'The power of trust in manufacturer-retailer relationships', *Harvard Business Review Influence* (November), .

LLC, T.B.G. (2008) 'The power of personal responsibility', Available at: http://brendonburchard.tumblr.com/post/88770370853/the-power-of-personal-responsibility (Accessed: 29 August 2016).

Mehrabian, A. (1972) *Silent messages: Implicit communication of emotions and attitudes.* Belmont, CA, United States: Belmont, Calif., Wadsworth Pub. Co. [1971].

Schwartz, T. and Loehr, J.E. (2004) *The power of full engagement: Managing energy, not time, is the key to high performance and personal renewal.* New York: Simon & Schuster Adult Publishing Group.

SMB Communications Study: Uncovering The Hidden Costs of Communications Barriers And Latency (2010) Available at: http://about.pdpsolutions.com/bm.doc/smb_communications_study.pdf (Accessed: 29 August 2016).

BIBLIOGRAPHY
(Continued)

Statistics About Strategic Planning (no date) Available at: http://missionfacilitators.com/wp-content/uploads/2013/03/Statistics-About-Strategic-Planning.pdf (Accessed: 29 August 2016).

Technologies, R. (2016) 'The cost of poor internal communication', Available at: https://www.retrieve.com/blog/internal-communication (Accessed: 29 August 2016).

The Cost of Workplace Conflict (2003) HR Magazine (February), .

ThomasAs, D. (2016) 'Guideposts classics: Danny Thomas on keeping his promise', *Guideposts* (January), .

ABOUT THE AUTHOR

Gary Wilbers has been an entrepreneur and owner of multiple businesses in Missouri since 1990. He created an acronym that has

"I help coach individuals and organizations to Ascend to their peak in their personal and professional life, so they can achieve their dreams, goals and ambitions."

shaped his life's foundation: **CHARGE** (Create Habits Around Real Goals Everyday). He studied entrepreneurs such as Sam Walton, Brendon Burchard, Brian Tracy, and Charles Red Scott and learned their principles. Then he built his roadmap for personal success.

The first business Gary built, Mid-America Wireless, started as a small two-man company and culminated with ten regional storefronts and over one hundred fifty employees. He developed a culture of learning and sharing knowledge within his organizations. His goal and commitment was to always make a team member better equipped than when he/she started. Gary created a framework, The High Achiever Mindset, using his success as the foundation. He now shares his message as a keynote speaker, trainer, and coach in order to help others reach their goals, dreams, and ambitions. He is a certified High Performance Coach from the High Performance Institute.

Gary is also involved in his community and gives his time and resources to several organizations. His passion is working with Special Olympics Missouri. He currently serves on the statewide board and is the Capital Campaign Chair for the Training for Life Campus fund drive with the purpose of building a state of the art facility for Missouri athletes. One of his greatest joys is playing unified golf with Keith Lueckenhoff, a SOMO athlete. Gary and his wife Dana have three children, Chris, Adam and Elle, and reside in Wardsville, MO.

HOW TO CONTACT GARY

For more information on Coaching, Training, and Keynote Speaking, contact Gary and the Ascend Team:

Phone: (573) 644-6655 or (866) 549-0434

Email: GWilbers@GoAscend.biz

Online: www.goascend.biz

Gary Wilbers
1731 Elm Court
Jefferson City, MO 65101

Subscribe to Gary's weekly video blog:

www.goascend.biz/blog/

To purchase bulk copies of this book at a discounted rate, please contact Gary Wilbers:

gwilbers@goascend.biz or (573) 644-6655

MEET THE ASCEND TEAM

Ascend Business Strategies began because Gary wanted better training with more complete Human Resources and Leadership Development opportunities for his companies. Through its early development stage, it became very evident this was soon to be an organization that could help other businesses with training resources designed for practical use and address what is not commonly taught in business management schools. The desire to help others develop and become better launched a national business based in the heart of Missouri.

To learn more about coaching, keynote speaking, and our unique training programs, contact Ascend Business Strategies at goascend.biz or (866) 549-0434.

Gary Wilbers is a High Performance Coach, Speaker, and Trainer. He works with organizations to transform the challenges leaders and teams face in regards to change and growth. Gary has been a successful entrepreneur and owner of multiple businesses in Missouri since 1990. He studied entrepreneurs such as Sam Walton, Brendon Burchard, Brian Tracy, and Charles Red Scott. He learned their principles and then built his own roadmap for success which he shares as he helps leaders develop into High Achievers.

Rod Long is a Business Coach, Trainer, Product Developer, and Speaker for Ascend Business Strategies. He has been in the fields of Leadership and Team Development, Coaching, Ministry, Business Mentoring, and Facilitating for over twenty years. He is a published author and has successfully trained and developed some of today's top leaders. Influencers in his life include John Maxwell, Stephen Covey, Peter Drucker, and Brendon Burchard.

VIDEO SERIES FOR READERS OF THE HIGH ACHIEVER LEADERSHIP FORMULA

Retail Value of $197

Special High Achiever's Offer **ONLY $47**
Use Promo Code: 150BOOK

http://goascend.biz/savenow

The difference between a leader who gains commitment from others and one who only gains compliance is coaching.

Access Coaching for Success:

- **5 In-Depth Training Modules**
- **Downloadable Resources**
- **Lifetime Access*** for You & Your Team

http://goascend.biz/savenow

How to engage and empower your team in the workplace:

Think back on your life. Who has been the most inspiring and influential? What attributes did he/she display when interacting with those around him/her? What made this person significant to you? As you examine his/her actions, you will likely find the skills described in this book were displayed consistently in his/her day-to-day life. Often, these individuals learned early that when you invest in others to help them obtain their goals, dreams and desires, you then achieve your own goals.

Claim your exclusive offer now!

http://goascend.biz/savenow

*Access as long as Ascend Business Strategies is in operation.